If These
WALLS
Could TALK:
MILWAUKEE BREWERS

If These **WALLS** *Could* **TALK:**
MILWAUKEE BREWERS

Stories from the
Milwaukee Brewers Dugout,
Locker Room, and Press Box

Bill Schroeder with Drew Olson

TRIUMPH
B O O K S

Library of Congress Cataloging-in-Publication Data
Names: Schroeder, Bill, 1958- author. | Olson, Drew, 1966- author.
Title: If these walls could talk : Milwaukee Brewers : stories from the Milwaukee Brewers dugout, locker room, and press box / by Bill Schroeder with Drew Olson.
Description: Chicago, Illinois : Triumph Books LLC, [2016]
Identifiers: LCCN 2015042304 | ISBN 9781629372037
Subjects: LCSH: Milwaukee Brewers (Baseball team)—History. | Milwaukee Brewers (Baseball team)—Anecdotes.
Classification: LCC GV875.M53 S34 2016 | DDC 796.357/640977595—dc23
LC record available at http://lccn.loc.gov/2015042304

This book is available in quantity at special discounts for your group or organization. For further information, contact:

Triumph Books LLC
814 North Franklin Street
Chicago, Illinois 60610
(312) 337–0747
www.triumphbooks.com

Printed in U.S.A.

ISBN: 978-1-62937-203-7

Design by Amy Carter

Photos courtesy of Associated Press unless otherwise indicated

*To my mother and father, who gave up a lot of summer vacations
to drive me to baseball tournaments, and to my wife, Kate, and
my three children—daughters, Lindsey and Mallory, and son, Billy—
for allowing me to spend so much time at the ballpark*

CONTENTS

Foreword *by Craig Counsell*..xi

Foreword *by Bob Uecker*..xv

Introduction..xix

Part I: Brewers Greats 1
This Bud's for You, Robin Yount, Paul Molitor,
Bob Uecker

Part II: Smorgasbord of Stories 51
Food, Team Parties, The Chandler Explosion,
The Sausage Race, Nicknames

Part III: Great Games..83
Brewers Win the 1982 Pennant; Tony Plush Saves the
Day; Braun and CC Brew Up a Winner; It Takes 162;
Good-bye, Detroit; The Kid Hits 3,000; Molitor's Streak
Ends; Shadow Dancing; County Stadium Finale; Grand
Salami; The Hit Parade; The Future Arrives; Friday Night
Fights; May Marathon; Nieves' No-Hitter; CC's Near
No-No; Easter Sunday '87

Part IV: Behind the Scenes 115

Director of Clubhouse Operations, Clubhouse Pranks,
The Training Room, The Video Revolution, Team Travel,
Batting Practice

Part V: In the Booth 185

My Baseball Life, Becoming a Broadcaster, Matt Vasgersian,
Daron Sutton, Brian Anderson, Director, Producer, Calling
Pitches

Acknowledgments...223

Sources 227

FOREWORD

It's hard to believe that Bill Schroeder is in his third decade broadcasting Brewers games on TV. He's certainly aged as a beautiful man, but 20-plus years is a long time. There is a generation of Brewers fans who have learned about baseball from watching Bill Schroeder. The fans know who he is. I think what people realize—more than anything—when they watch Bill is that he's a Brewer. That certainly lends something to the broadcast.

I know that once you step into the booth, you have to try to be impartial because you're telling the story of the game. But it also comes through that Bill was a Brewer as a player and now as a broadcaster. He's been through good times and bad. He has lived the history of the franchise, and that comes through, and that makes everybody more passionate. Because of that fans can share their love for the team more. The fact that Bill was a player gives him perspective. He can explain certain situations and tell fans how players feel and how they are reacting and how they're anticipating. That's a difficult thing to do for someone who didn't play the game.

Bill provides those insights. He does a great job with it. But I also know—after watching and listening to him over the years—that he demands a lot of the players and also understands how hard it is to play. That's a good combination, and it seems to come naturally for him.

I did a little bit of TV work after I retired as a player, and there is an adrenaline that you don't always get when you're done playing. It's hard to replace the excitement on the field, but you get a bit of that in the broadcast booth. You are on live TV and living the game, and the challenge of it is a rush. The joy of coming to the park and performing comes out every day. In that way it's similar to playing.

The link between Rock and the fans, though, goes beyond the games. He runs the team's fantasy camps and does a really good job with it. I know the former players love going down there, and the campers come back and everybody has a blast, and the stories are really great. It's another way, in addition to his charitable activities and work with military groups, that Bill is representing the Brewers, and he's representing them in the right way.

Bill was with the Brewers in the 1980s and played with some of the best players in franchise history—Robin Yount, Paul Molitor, Jim Gantner, Ted Simmons, Rollie Fingers, and others. That's still such an important era for the Brewers. So many fans associate that with their childhood, and the fact that he was part of that is important. He provides a link to that, but he's also been around great players as a broadcaster, guys like Ryan Braun, Prince Fielder, Jonathan Lucroy, Carlos Gomez, CC Sabathia, and Zack Greinke. There are a bunch of fans who identify with those guys. Bill has been a link to that group, too.

For the next great Brewers team, he can provide a link to those guys. He is able to do that and he does a good job of it. And I think people are going to enjoy reading his stories because his story really is intertwined with the story of the Brewers.

—*Craig Counsell*

FOREWORD

You want me to say something about Bill? *Bill who? Bill Schroeder?* Never heard of him…

I'm kidding, of course.

I think Rock and I have always been close, going back to when he played for the Brewers in the early 1980s. Now that he's a broadcaster, we talk to each other every day for the most part. I was always kind of partial to catchers anyway because that's what I did, too, as a player.

Rock was a good catcher. He hit with some power and he was a good receiver, too. He also was a big dude. That's one thing that always impressed me with Rock. He was a big guy who never shied from anything.

We talked a lot when he was playing, but we do it even more now that he's working in the broadcast part of baseball. We talk about what goes on in the field and what goes on in the broadcast booth. It's nice that he asks me a lot of times for tips on the broadcast part.

Once you have the separation from player to broadcasting, there are some guys who don't want to talk to you anymore. That's fine. But I think players know that we're going to be fair. Rock knows the intricacies of the game. He knows why things happen, which is what you get from playing.

We like to have fun and make people laugh, but we don't ever rip guys just to rip them and we don't mess around when we've got a good game going. I've talked to Rock about that a lot. He gets it. There is a comfort zone for him with fans. Broadcasting for a team is not easy. It's not like doing a network game, where you can say whatever you want. You have seasons where it's sometimes hard to watch. But when you work for a particular team, you get a closeness with the players and the people in the organization.

I've been around long enough now that I've seen guys as players. I've seen their kids. And now, I've seen their grandkids. When you look at Robin (Yount), Paulie (Molitor), Cecil Cooper, Jim Gantner, Gorman

Thomas—those guys have been the foundation for what we have here today in Milwaukee. They never go away. When you do see them—either at a Brewers On Deck event in the winter or someplace else—it's like old home week. You really enjoy being around the guys. People move on at times to different teams. That's part of the game. But you never lose that connection, and I know that Billy likes that part of it a lot. I never wanted to leave here. There were opportunities over the years, but I never wanted to leave here. I'm a Brewer.

Bill is a Brewer, too. He does fantasy camp every year. He asked me if I'd spend a day in fantasy camp. I said, "Sure, absolutely." I'm happy to do that. That's still a big connection. Bill didn't leave after he was done as a player and hung around Wisconsin. He will be here for a long, long time, however long he wants to be. There is a comfort zone for Bill with fans and the organization. He is a great fit.

—*Bob Uecker*

INTRODUCTION

Growing up, I played in all kinds of sports. I played football, basketball, soccer, but baseball was my favorite. My first exposure to baseball came through my father. He was a junior high baseball coach, helping kids feed into Steinert High School in Hamilton Township in New Jersey. I remember going to practices and games with my father as a really young kid. I'd be around collecting balls in the outfield and picking up bats and things like that and I developed an instant love for the game.

When I was about seven years old, they didn't have T-ball or anything like that. We just started playing. When I signed up for my first team, they called it the "Tiny League" back then. I was seven and playing against eight and nine-year olds. I remember going to registration at the fire house in Hamilton. I was standing with my dad. There were a couple of men at the desk, and there was a lady making sure we lived where we said we did and that we had the proper forms filled out. While my dad was getting me signed up, I looked around and saw an old cardboard box—it was probably an empty beer case—and there was some catcher's gear in there. I knew what it was because I had been hanging around the ballpark during my dad's practices. The catcher's gear was heavy and dirty, and it took a long time for players to put on and take off and it was hard to stuff into the equipment bag at the end of the day. I didn't want anything to do with it.

As we were getting ready to walk out, I pointed to the box and told my dad, "I don't want to wear that stuff. I don't ever want to play catcher." He said, "Don't worry about it. Don't worry about it. We'll take care of it."

A little while later, we had our first practice. The first one I ever went to, and they strapped the gear on me and put me behind the plate. My father said, "You're going to thank me some day..."

Lo and behold, I was a catcher from that day forward.

(Courtesy: Milwaukee Brewers)

PART I:
BREWERS GREATS

This Bud's for You

People often ask me, "What was it like to work for Bud Selig?" I tell them it was great and I mean it.

When I first got to the big leagues, Bud wasn't the commissioner yet. He was around a lot, and we would talk to him. Every once in a while, when things were going rough, he would come down and let us have it. He didn't do that often, but you could tell that he cared deeply about the team. He would come and watch batting practice, and you'd see him with that Tiparillo cigar and you could tell the ballpark was where he was happy.

When I got called up, I could tell right away that he had a special relationship with the guys from the 1982 team—Robin, Paulie, Rollie, and others. He loved those guys.

When I first came up, Harvey Kuenn was managing and his wife, Audrey, was around the club a lot, and so were Bud and his wife, Sue Selig. It was really a family atmosphere. It felt like a mom and pop store in some ways. Audrey was referred to as "Mom." She loved the players, and they loved her.

Although we always called him "Mr. Selig," he wasn't an intimidating figure. He would do things for us. He had the car dealership at the time. If you wanted a car, word got out and you'd go see Bud. I would go see his secretary, Lori Keck, an amazing lady who also worked for legendary Packers coach Vince Lombardi, and tell her I needed to talk to Mr. Selig. I would go into his office, which looked exactly like it does in the Selig Experience—down to the piles of newspapers on the floor, and we would work out a deal.

He used to give players interest-free loans with payments taken out of our checks to buy cars. He didn't have to do that, but he did. He was very generous that way. The best way I can describe the whole atmosphere at that time was that it was like a family business. When it was someone's birthday, there would be cards, cake, and other treats. There were holiday parties. One time, I had a team party at my house and just about everybody showed up and I was stunned to see Bud show up. I probably shouldn't have been surprised because that's the kind of boss he was. But if I had known he was coming, I would have cut my grass.

I know a lot of people will remember Bud most for his work as commissioner. He was a consensus builder. He came in at a tough time with the work stoppages and the strike that prompted him to cancel the World Series in 1994. He dealt with the steroid issue in the late 1990s and 2000s. He worked through realignment with the Brewers moving to the National League and the Astros later moving to the American League and he instituted the wild-card, which has been a huge success.

As successful as he was in the commissioner's office, I'll always think of Bud in his role with the Brewers. The one thing I tell people is that he was the ultimate fan. When I played we could see him pacing on the loge out in front of the press box. It was right at the top of the screen, and there would be media guys up there and we could see him pace.

Bud's private box was located right next to the press box. Reporters always told us how he would come in and chat when the game was going well. His door was metal, and when things were going south for the Brewers, you often heard the door slam with a loud bang that shook the press box. When it got tight, he would pace. We could see him do it. When we had a bad inning, he would slam the door to his private box, walk into the press box, banter with reporters, and slam the door on his way out. Then he'd go back to his box and slam the door again. Tom Haudricourt from the *Milwaukee Journal Sentinel* still laughs about the "triple slam" moments.

I remember one day during spring training I popped into the manager's office to chat with Phil Garner because we were getting ready to broadcast a Cactus League game to the folks back in Wisconsin. The team hadn't been playing very well at that time, but…it was spring training, so nobody seemed too upset about it.

Well, one person was.

As Phil and I were chatting with a couple of writers, Bud walked by. He had just arrived from Milwaukee and he wasn't thrilled. "I've been around long enough to know that the outcome down here doesn't really matter in the big picture," Selig said, smiling. "It would be nice, though, if we could win *once in a while*. We're trying to sell tickets back home. Any help you can give us in that regard would be greatly appreciated."

The next day, with the game on TV, Phil trotted out his A team. He played a bunch of starters, and the Brewers fell behind by five runs in the first inning. I'm not sure if Bud slammed any doors that day, but I'm sure he wanted to.

Bud's rapport with the press was legendary. He liked newspapers and had a pretty good grasp on the concept that free publicity was good even when the stories weren't all that rosy. There was a lot of good-natured ripping between him and the men of the Fourth Estate. Bud Lea, a long-time columnist for the *Milwaukee Sentinel*, was one of his favorite targets. Bud spent a lot of time covering the Green Bay Packers, and when he would show up at the ballpark in August, Bud Selig would say, "Hey Bud Lea, shouldn't you be covering a Packers scrimmage?" Bud acted like the Packers were competition, but he loved them almost as much as he loved the Brewers. He and Henry Aaron used to go to games together, and he served for a time on the Packers board of directors.

The press box at County Stadium was pretty cozy. Visiting writers sat in the second row and would howl with laughter at some of the barbs traded between Bud and the local writers. One year, the Brewers had a problem when a skunk built a nest under the stands near the home bullpen. They actually brought in animal control to trap the critter, and it became one of those light local news stories that TV stations like to deliver to viewers.

Haudricourt wasn't about to let that one slip by. "Hey, Bud, I don't see what the big deal is about the skunk," he said. "I've been writing stories all season saying that your bullpen stinks." In most cases, Bud would have shot back with something about the quality of Tom's writing or the general state of the newspaper and Journal Company stock, but this time he smiled.

Like many owners Bud had his favorite players. But he was such a big fan that he often rode a roller coaster. In the mid-1990s, the Brewers had an outfielder named Gerald Williams, who was acquired with Wisconsin native Bob Wickman in a deal that sent Pat Listach, Graeme Lloyd, and later Ricky Bones to the New York Yankees. A few weeks into Williams' tenure in Milwaukee, Selig popped into the press box just as Williams delivered a base hit. "You know, I really like this Williams kid," Selig gushed. "He really plays the game the right way."

A few innings later, Selig was back in the press box, probably grabbing another Diet Coke, when Williams—who had failed to execute a sacrifice bunt and then struck out to short-circuit a rally—missed a cutoff man and allowed a runner to grab an extra base.

"I don't know what the hell Williams is doing tonight," Selig said. "He looks awful."

"But Bud, you were just singing his praises," Haudricourt said.

"I know what I said, but he's terrible right now."

As so often happens in baseball, Williams redeemed himself. He made a nice catch in the outfield and delivered another hit. When the game ended and the Brewers were exchanging congratulatory handshakes on the field and writers were heading to the clubhouse for postgame interviews, Selig stopped Haudricourt and said, "I know what I said before, but I really do like Williams."

One of the all-time classic Selig press box stories ended up inspiring the title of a book. During one particularly ugly game, Brewers media relations director Tom Skibosh and his assistant, Mario Ziino, were laughing about a joke someone had told or something that happened in a fantasy football draft or something like that when Selig stormed in and caught them laughing at what he felt should have been a somber moment. "If you want to have fun, go someplace else!" he bellowed, before storming out of the press box, slamming doors along the way.

Silence fell over the tiny press box until Haudricourt, once described by Toronto writer Bob Elliott as "the Archenemy of Silence," piped up. "You know, he's right," Haudricourt said. "If we want to have fun, we should go someplace. In fact, that would probably be a good marketing slogan for the team next year."

Everybody cracked up. After being downsized during the 1994 work stoppage, Skibosh ended up writing a memoir and calling it, *If You Wanna Have Fun, Go Someplace Else.*

* * *

One of the more magical evenings of the 2015 season took place on May 28 at Miller Park. Unfortunately, the Brewers were off that night. (It was one of those years). May 28 was the night that the club unveiled "the Selig Experience." Tucked into a corner of the left-field loge level, the Selig Experience is a state-of-the-art multimedia presentation that chronicles Milwaukee baseball history and the career of the former Brewers president and Major League Baseball commissioner. It wasn't until I went through the exhibit for the first time that I realized how intertwined the two entities are.

The guest list for the debut party, an elegant affair held on an unseasonably warm summer night in center field, was impressive. Henry Aaron, a close friend of Selig for 50 years, was on hand along with Robin Yount, Bob Uecker, and University of Wisconsin athletic director Barry Alvarez. Selig's successor as commissioner, Rob Manfred, was on hand as was his special assistant, Joe Torre, who began his big league career playing for the Milwaukee Braves. Jeff Idelson, the president of the National Baseball Hall of Fame and Museum, was in the crowd as was Rachael and Sharon Robinson, the widow and daughter of one of Selig's heroes, Jackie Robinson.

The Brewers had already dedicated a statue to Selig outside Miller Park, where his likeness is immortalized near Aaron and Yount, his two favorite Milwaukee players. They also retired uniform No. 1 to honor their No. 1 fan. The Selig Experience, which was conceived by then-general manager Doug Melvin and designed by BRC Imagination Arts, which had experience with presidential libraries and several iconic brands like Ford, Coca-Cola, Guinness, Disney, and others, really is a must-see for Brewers fans of all ages. The video display, which lasts less than 15 minutes, gives way to a re-creation of Selig's County Stadium office (complete with his trademark Tiparillo cigar emitting a trail of smoke from an ashtray) and ends with a hologram of the man himself addressing the audience. "All the talent in the world, all the most incredible technology in the world is meaningless without a great story," said Brad Shelton, the creative director of BRC, at a press conference following the unveiling. "And, man, did we have a great story." Shelton and his team were struck by the fact that Selig's story is interwoven with Milwaukee's baseball history. "It's very rare that we get to work on something that has this kind of importance to the city which it's in," he said.

Speaking to reporters on the field, Manfred echoed that sentiment. "It is an amazing tribute to an amazing man and a great career, particularly that portion of his career that was spent here in Milwaukee," he said. "Some of us who worked with Bud for years in New York focus on all he accomplished as commissioner, and we forget, lose track of the fact, that he was the person that saved baseball in Milwaukee."

As I sat in the intimate theater, which features three rows of bleachers and three floor-to-ceiling video screens, I watched the story of Bud's love affair with the game unfold. It began when his mother, a Russian immigrant named Marie, who was an elementary school teacher, took him to games at Milwaukee's Borchert Field, home of the American Association, and to New York baseball shrines like Yankee Stadium, Ebbets Field, and the Polo Grounds.

When the Braves came to Milwaukee in 1953, Selig was in college and he was a dedicated fan. As a college student at the University of Wisconsin, he attended the Braves' first game on April 14, 1953, and saw Warren Spahn pitch and become a winner when Billy Bruton hit a game-winning homer in the bottom of the 10th inning. "When Billy Bruton hit the home run off [St. Louis Cardinals outfielder] Enos Slaughter's glove to win the game, it was wild," he recalled. "It became a love affair with the intensity that no one could have predicted."

Selig was a graduate student in the fall of 1957, skipping an accounting class in Madison to watch the Braves clinch the pennant on Aaron's homer off St. Louis pitcher Billy Muffett. "My seat was right behind a post, but I was there, and it was one of the most exciting nights of my life," Selig said. "I remembered that a lot more than anything I would have learned in that accounting class, I can tell you that."

When the Braves left Milwaukee for Atlanta in 1965, Selig was devastated and determined to keep baseball in his hometown. He formed a group called Teams Inc. and sued to keep the Braves from leaving. The lawsuit failed, so Selig shifted his focus. With local businessmen like Ed Fitzgerald, Bob Uihlein, Irv Maier, and Ben Barkin behind him, Selig formed Milwaukee Brewers Baseball Club Inc. and began trying to get an expansion franchise.

Though the Braves had been successful on the field and at the gate—at least until crowds dwindled during their lame-duck year—Selig met resistance from other owners because of his previous lawsuit. "There was plenty of anger, and I can understand that," he said. "They weren't happy with us, but they also knew that Milwaukee was an incredible baseball town. The Braves were the first National League team to draw 2 million fans. The fans were so passionate. But it was an uphill battle."

At the major league owner's meeting on May 27, 1968, in Chicago, National League president Warren Giles stepped to the microphone to announce two expansion franchises. "I saw the 'M' forming in his mouth and my heart jumped," Selig recalled. "I was sure he was going to say 'Milwaukee.'" To Selig's dismay, the National League welcomed Montreal to the big leagues. San Diego received the other NL bid with Kansas City and Seattle joining the American League. Once again, many people thought Milwaukee's bid was dead. Selig soldiered on. "It was the toughest five-year period in my life," he said. "I learned a lot of lessons about perseverance and tenacity."

With the expansion dream extinguished, Selig set his sights on buying an existing team. He tried to lure the Chicago White Sox to town, even welcoming the South Siders for a few well-attended exhibitions, but the American League nixed the sale. "Time was running out," Selig said. "Even people close to me were telling me to give up. We were down to our last chance."

In 1970 the Seattle Pilots filed for bankruptcy after one failed season at Sick's Stadium. Selig made a bid to buy the team and ended up getting it for just less than $11 million. "I cried when I got the news," Selig said. "I didn't think it was going to happen." There wasn't much time to celebrate. As spring training ended, the Pilots equipment truck stopped in Las Vegas to await orders to continue to Washington or Wisconsin. Selig had to hire a staff and be ready for the home opener in a week.

On April 7, 1970, a crowd of 37,237 gathered at County Stadium as Lew Krause and the Brewers dropped a 12–0 decision to the California Angels and Andy Messersmith. "It's the only time in my career that I didn't care whether we won or lost," Selig said. "I was so happy to have a team in Milwaukee, and we had so many things to take care of that it didn't matter. I'll never forget, though, as I was walking to my office after the final out a woman came up to me and said, 'You wanted a team in the worst way, and that's exactly what you got.' I never forgot that."

Slowly but surely, the Brewers began to improve the on-field product. Video from the Selig Experience chronicles the exploits of "Bambi's Bombers" and "Harvey's Wallbangers." I defy Brewers fans to watch highlights of Yount, Paul Molitor, Gorman Thomas, Cecil Cooper, Jim Gantner, Sixto Lezcano, Mike Caldwell, Rollie Fingers, Ted Simmons, and others and not get chills.

I know I did, especially the part about "Team Streak" in 1987. I was around for the 13-game winning streak to start the season, Juan Nieves' no-hitter, and Paul Molitor's 39-game hitting streak. I also got chills watching highlights from the playoff runs in 2008 and 2011. "There are a lot of lessons to be learned in the great story of the Milwaukee Brewers," Selig said at the Experience gala. "What they meant, what they mean today. All the ups and downs. And they're all chronicled there. I hope that people that come [to the Experience] will really understand the franchise, what it means, what it will mean in the future, and what we went through to get it and keep it."

Though Selig became acting commissioner in 1992 and began turning over operation of the club to his daughter, Wendy Selig-Prieb, he did find one more occasion to beat the odds. In the early 1990s, when it became apparent that the Brewers wouldn't be able to compete against bigger market clubs without a new stadium, Selig led the battle to build Miller Park.

The situation was similar to what some saw as a Quixotic battle to bring baseball back to Milwaukee in the late 1970s. With resistance popping up at nearly every turn, including some behind-the-scenes obstructionism from politicians who purported to be supporters, Selig plowed forward. He enlisted Aaron and Yount to lobby legislators. On October 6, 1995, a financing measure passed 16–15, when George Petak of Racine switched his vote in the final hour. Construction of Miller Park, which was delayed by a tragic crane accident in 1999 that claimed the lives of iron workers Jeffrey Wischer, William DeGrave, and Jerome Starr, wrapped up in time for the season opener in 2001. Milwaukee hosted the All-Star Game in 2002 and will host big-league baseball in retractable-roof comfort for years to come.

Bud Selig had preserved baseball in Milwaukee, a feat almost as unlikely as bringing it back in the first place. "Of all the marvelous things that have happened to me, including becoming commissioner of baseball, that will always be my proudest accomplishment because the odds were stacked tremendously against us," Selig said. "There were many times when I wondered if it would happen."

Robin Yount

People often ask if I have a favorite story about Robin Yount, who I was lucky enough to play with for six of the 20 seasons he spent in Milwaukee on his way to the National Baseball Hall of Fame and Museum in Cooperstown, New York.

I don't have a favorite Robin Yount story. I have hundreds of them.

I could talk about his incredible hand-eye coordination. I could talk about his speed and strength. I could gush about the way he ran out every ground ball or the discipline he showed by refusing to give away an at-bat despite the score or situation. I could tell you how he moved from the toughest infield position—shortstop—to the toughest outfield position—center field—without a complaint or a drop-off in production. I could talk about his swing, which allowed him to hit for power and average. We could chat about his laid-back manner, his wry sense of humor, and love of motorcycles and golf. We could talk about the way he led by example, the fun that he had goofing around with Jim Gantner and others.

But if you asked me to tell one story to sum up Robin Yount, I'd go with one I heard from Tony Migliaccio, the longtime director of clubhouse operations. One day while moving some things around in a storage area at County Stadium, Migliaccio discovered a box that contained Yount's Silver Slugger Award, a silver bat mounted on a black base. "I figured Robin would want it," Migliaccio said. "So I asked him if he wanted me to send it to his house in Arizona. He said, 'You don't have to go through the trouble. Why don't you just keep it?'"

That's Robin in a nutshell. He didn't care about awards, accolades, or articles in the newspapers and magazines. All he cared about was playing the game as hard as he could and trying to win. I lived near him during my time with the Brewers and I would stop by his house sometimes to drop something off, and he'd be cutting his grass, cleaning the pool, or playing with his kids. He was just a normal Wisconsin guy, who happened to be one of the best baseball players on the planet.

The Brewers drafted Yount with the third pick in the 1973 draft. Only David Clyde (Rangers) and John Stearns (Phillies) were taken ahead of Yount, who was a standout at Taft High School in Southern California. The player taken behind him was Dave Winfield, another future Hall of Famer. (It's the only time in history that Hall of Famers were selected with back-to-back picks in the first round.) Yount's high school coach, Ray O'Connor, called him "the standard by which most high school players are judged. I don't know of anyone in the same category," O'Connor told the *Los Angeles Times* in the late 1980s. "Lots of times there were as many scouts in the stands when we played as there were fans. He had that kind of talent."

Although he got a bigger kick from riding dirt bikes than playing baseball, Yount's talent was evident. He learned the game with help from his older brother, Larry, who used to throw him batting practice in the yard. Selected by Houston in the fifth round of the 1968 draft, Larry worked his way through Rookie Ball and Class A and was invited to big league camp. In September of 1971, he got the call to the big leagues. On September 15—a day before Robin turned 16—he was called from the bullpen to pitch the ninth inning of a game against the Braves.

With a crowd of 6,513 looking on at the Astrodome, Yount began warming up for his big league debut. His elbow, which had bothered him in the bullpen, began to ache with each pitch. It wasn't nerves. It

Robin Yount celebrates winning the 1982 American League Championship Series against the Baltimore Orioles.

was pain. He called out to his catcher. The trainer came out. He couldn't pitch. He left the mound that day and never returned to the major leagues. Less than two years later, the Brewers took Robin. He signed for $65,000, which he later said felt like "megabucks." After playing 64 games for Newark of the Class A New York-Penn League, where he hit .285, Yount received an invitation to big league spring training the following year.

In typical Yount fashion, he didn't think it was a big deal. He kept waiting to be sent to the minor leagues, but Brewers manager Del Crandall had other ideas. "The first time I even looked at him—I hadn't even noticed him, you know he only had 60 games, I think, in rookie ball—and so I just happened to be standing behind the batting cage one day and looked out, and one of the coaches was hitting him fungoes at shortstop," Crandall told the *Milwaukee Sentinel* years later. "I saw this lanky kid, and he had good range and good hands, and we had a terrible field, and that ball would bounce up and hit him in the shoulder, and he'd go over and pick it up and toss it in and get another one. And so I went over to the coach and said let me hit him some. Robin was about at the end of his workout, and I hit him some more ground balls and he just looked like he had that great makeup and obvious talent. He could throw, he had good range, and, like I say, he had good hands. And nobody knows whether they can hit or not until they get the opportunity. So I went to my general manager, who was Jim Wilson, and I asked him if there was any reason why an 18-year-old kid could not start on our ballclub...I said I want to play him. I think we had about 15 games left on our spring training schedule. I said I want to play him every day and see how he handles the 0-for-4s and how he handles the boots and he handles some adversity. And he was just tremendous. He had just great, great makeup. So he started the season with us. It was just that obvious that he could play and then it was just a matter of could he play at a major league level enough so he could gain confidence and help the ballclub, and he could do that."

Yount was the Brewers' starting shortstop on Opening Day and was the youngest player in the majors through his second season. Though he hit around .250 and averaged 30 errors in each of his first three seasons, Yount became a fan favorite on a team that began to hit its stride in the late 1970s. By the time the Brewers became playoff contenders in the early '80s, Yount, who had boosted his strength with an offseason work-out program, was regarded by players and managers as one of the best players in the game. Outside of Milwaukee, however, few people knew who he was. "If he had played in New York or Los Angeles, he would have been God," teammate Charlie Moore told the *Milwaukee Journal Sentinel.* Yount had no desire to play in a bigger market. "He'd have been miserable in New York or Boston," former trainer John Adam said. "He would have hated the attention."

When you think about the fact that Yount won two MVP awards (as a shortstop in 1982 and a center fielder in 1989) and played in only three All-Star Games in his career, it is pretty remarkable. Cal Ripken Jr. of Baltimore became a dominant shortstop. Rickey Henderson and Kirby Puckett were the stars in the outfield. But Yount couldn't even get a bench spot? Again, he didn't care. Flying under the radar suited him fine. "When I was drafted by the Brewers, I really didn't know much about the organization, but when I went to Milwaukee, it was a place I really enjoyed from the very start," Yount said during his Hall of Fame induction weekend. "It was just a perfect fit for me and my family. I enjoyed every bit of going back there. Not just the baseball, but the people and what Wisconsin had to offer—with the exception of the winters; I didn't spend any of them back there. It is just a place that, between the way I was treated back there, which was unbelievable...it's just a place I really enjoy going."

At age 26 in 1982, Yount put up one of the best seasons in base-ball history. He hit .331. He belted 29 homers, drove in a 114 runs, and scored 129. He led the league in hits (210), doubles (46), total bases

(367), and slugging percentage (.578) and won a Gold Glove at short. In the final game of the regular season, the Brewers played a do-or-die game in Baltimore. Both teams entered the day with 94–67 records. The winner would go to the American League Championship Series. The loser would head to the golf course.

Facing future Hall of Famer and Orioles pitcher Jim Palmer, Yount homered in his first at-bat. He homered again later and tripled. He scored four runs and the Brewers, behind a solid outing by future Hall of Famer Don Sutton, won the game 10–2. The only downside for Yount came in the ninth inning. When Dennis Martinez hit him with a pitch, he ended up one hit away from winning the batting title. "He's not all-league or even All-American," Sutton said. "He's all-world. I've played with a lot of great players, but Robin Yount is the best all-around player I've ever seen."

The Brewers lost a seven-game World Series against the St. Louis Cardinals, but Yount made an impression with a pair of four-hit games, a .414 batting average, and an epic motorcycle ride around the warning track at the team's almost-victory celebration at County Stadium. Shoulder problems prompted Yount to move to center field in 1985. In 1989 he won his second MVP award after hitting .318 with 21 homers, 103 RBIs, and 101 runs scored and 19 steals.

"He was the best player I ever saw," Gorman Thomas said. "Other people may disagree, but I watched him play every day for 10 years. He could do everything. He was the total package."

Another element in that package was Yount's toughness. "Robin was old school, which is a cliché and a term that's overused," Adam recalled. "He overcame serious injuries, but he didn't get hurt that often. When he was a shortstop, he had a really bad shoulder. He had a labral tear, and there weren't a lot of doctors at that time who understood that injury. We sent him to Michigan to have surgery, and it was about a year before he was back able to throw okay. He also had a really serious low back injury in the early '80s. Back then, there was a short period of time that they injected stuff in your low back that they felt worked for some people. It was an enzyme, I think, derived from a pineapple or something. It was something weird. He got that. Two years later it was one of those things the medical field looks back on and goes, 'Yeah, that didn't work.' But he came back from that. He also had his knee scoped at the end of his career and he was on the 15-day disabled list, and I think he missed 19 days. Most guys take three or four weeks. He just thought, *Hey, I'm going to come back as soon as I can get off the DL. That's the way he was.*"

Yount didn't complain about injuries unless they kept him off the field. "I remember he broke a finger during the season one year and only missed a couple games," Adam said. "We went to get it X-rayed in Toronto, and he was yelling at me the whole time. He didn't think it was necessary. Well, the Blue Jays doctor did the X-ray and put it up on the light box, and even I could see the fracture. Robin yells, 'I told you it wasn't broken!' The doctor and I just looked at each other. We had to explain, 'Yes, it is a fracture.' He didn't miss more than three games."

Yount collected his 3,000th hit on September 9, 1992, at County Stadium, where he lined a pitch from Cleveland Indians pitcher Jose Mesa into right field and celebrated at first base with Paul Molitor and Gantner. Yount ended his career with 3,142 hits, 583 doubles, 126 triples, 251 homers, 1,406 RBIs, and 271 steals. He was elected to the Hall of Fame on the first ballot in 1998 and went in with his close friend, George Brett, and Nolan Ryan. Though he was always polite but not very talkative in media interviews during his playing days, Yount seemed to open up after retirement. His Hall of Fame induction speech was simple, classy, humorous, and a perfect summation of his career.

YOUNT INDUCTION SPEECH

Cooperstown, New York
July 26, 1999

You know, when I was a young boy I used to play baseball in my backyard or in the street with my brothers or the neighborhood kids. We used broken bats and plastic golf balls and played for hours and hours. My favorite team was the San Francisco Giants. And many of those players that were on that team are here today. I would try to pitch like Juan Marichal or Gaylord Perry and try to hit like Willie Mays, Orlando Cepeda, or Willie McCovey. After those games when I'd go home at night, oftentimes I would dream of being a major league player. I was lucky. That dream came true. I would dream of hitting a home run in a World Series or playing an All-Star Game. I was lucky those dreams came true. I had dreams of catching the ball for the final out in the World Series and being mobbed by my teammates. Well, I guess all my dreams didn't come true.

But what I'd really like to tell you is I never dreamed of being in the Hall of Fame. Standing here with all these great players was beyond any of my dreams. I can't begin to tell you what an honor it is to be up here with these guys. First of all I'd like to congratulate the other inductee—Bob Stevens on his award and the late Arch McDonald, Joe Williams, Frank Selee, and Nestor Chylak on their accomplishments.

You know, when I was 18 years old, I spent the day in a rowboat fishing with Nolan Ryan. There wasn't a lot of conversation that day. On the field he let his pitching do the talking. I never faced a pitcher with better stuff than Nolan Ryan. When I was 19, I went to Puerto Rico to play winter ball. And one of my teammates was Orlando Cepeda. He went out of his way to make a young kid a long way from home feel comfortable. It was certainly a great thrill to play with someone you used to imitate as a kid.

And George Brett. I think most people know that George and I have become pretty good friends over the years. But even before that, George was the guy I used to watch and say, "Man, I wish I could play like that guy." With a fun-loving attitude and a burning desire to win, nobody played the game any harder than George. He is what baseball is all about. I couldn't have handpicked a better class to go to Cooperstown with. Congratulations to all of you.

You know, no one ever accomplishes something like this without a lot of help from good people along the way. And this is certainly true in my case, and I would like to thank some of those people. When I started out in Little League, I was lucky enough to be drafted by a gentleman named Clem Cohen, who at the time I didn't know. He is a guy who knows and loves the game of baseball. He also knows and loves kids. Clem Cohen got me started on the right foot, and we still remain close friends today.

My high school coach was Ray O'Conner. He has coached a lot of players who have signed professional contracts, and many of those have gone on to play in the major leagues. In '73 I graduated high school and was lucky enough again to be drafted by the Milwaukee Brewers, a fairly new organization at the time, trying to establish itself in the American League. In spring training of '74, I went with the major league club, and the manager was Del Crandall. Fortunately, he saw enough potential from a raw 18-year-old kid to give me a chance. I am grateful for that.

And the hitting coach at the time was the late Harvey Kuenn, who a few years later became the manager of that club. Harvey and I developed a very close relationship early on, and that relationship grew with time. He taught me more about the game of baseball, both on and off the field, than anyone. I was also lucky to play for an owner, Bud Selig, who truly cared about his players. He'd call me into his office once in a while when he knew things weren't going so well. And it's funny. Every time I left there, I always felt that something good was about to happen.

You know over 20 years I played for a number of managers and dozens of coaches. I don't know any of them that I didn't learn something from to help make me a better player. But some of my favorites were George Bamberger, Frank Howard, Tom Trebelhorn, Sam Suplizio, Rene Lachemann, and Phil Garner. I was also very lucky to be a teammate of two of the greatest players to ever play the game. I learned very early on by playing for Frank Robinson and with Henry Aaron that even the greatest players in the game were just one of the guys. And without the many other teammates that I had over the years, none of this could have happened. Hitting around guys like Paul Molitor, Cecil Cooper, Ted Simmons, Gorman Thomas, Sal Bando, Larry Hisle, Ben Oglivie, just to name a few, certainly contributed to my career. And to have teammates like Rollie Fingers, Pete Vuckovich, Ed Sprague, Bob McClure, Moose Haas, Charlie Moore, Jimmy Gantner, Dale Sveum, Rob Deer, I could go on forever. But to have guys like this not only as teammates, but as friends made it where I couldn't wait to go to the ballpark every day.

And one of those guys, not exactly a teammate, but definitely one of the guys, he's here today—Bob Uecker. And believe it or not, Bob Uecker played a significant role in me being here today. My family, starting with my mom and dad. They were at every game when I was a kid. My mom would usually make me a pregame meal. She was always sewing up my torn uniform. She'd even play catch with me if I asked her to. My dad was always there, too. If I needed some batting practice, he was there to throw it to me. If I needed some ground balls, he was there to hit them to me. I could remember hanging a tarp from the swing set in the backyard, using it for a backstop. My dad would throw to me, and I'd hit the ball, and hopefully it would hit one of the walnut trees in the yard and stay in our yard. You know we lost a lot of balls that way.

My brother Larry. He taught me how hard work and dedication to the game was the only way to make it. He's taken care of all my business activities for me and my family for many years, and I thank him for that. My brother Jim, he's the light-hearted one. I never had to worry about getting a big head with him around. With his sense of humor, he always put me in my place. And to his wife, Cheryl, who's not feeling so well. They couldn't be here this weekend. Cheryl, you hang in there. We'll have our own party when I get home.

You know raising a family in the lifestyle of a professional athlete can be very difficult. I know during the baseball season I usually had blinders on to anything but the game. I took for granted that family matters would take care of themselves. Oftentimes I was there physically, but mentally my mind was always on the game. I realize now what a great job my wife, Michelle, did, not only in raising our children, Melissa, Amy, Dustin, and Jenna, but in taking care of me. And I love you all very much.

And to all my friends out there. Many of you have come a long way to be here today. And you fans out there, thank you for making this such an incredible day.

Okay, now is the time where I'm supposed to wake up from all of this. I mean, it's okay, it's been a great dream. But if in fact this is reality, then with all due respect, Mr. Gehrig, today I consider myself the luckiest man on the face of the earth.

Thank you.

You know, as great a day as this is for us up here, we have to remember there are people out there who are hurting. We are often reminded how quickly things can be taken from us. My heart goes out to the families of the men who lost their lives in the construction of the new stadium in Milwaukee. The game of life can sometimes be too short. So play it with everything you've got. Thank you very much.

Paul Molitor

It's only fitting that we follow a chapter on Robin Yount with a chapter on Paul Molitor. Whenever fans or former players talk about the Brewers of the 1980s, you hear "Robin and Paulie" or "Paulie and Robin." They were our rock stars. Like John Lennon and Paul McCartney of The Beatles, they were extremely talented, extremely different, and extremely popular with the fans. On playgrounds and sandlot fields across Wisconsin, kids would argue about who got to be Robin and who got to be Paul.

Both were first-round draft picks. Robin was a quiet California native, didn't like interviews very much, and had long, curly hair, and a bit of a "rock and roll" vibe. Paulie was from Minnesota, was classically handsome, was articulate, and comfortable enough in front of the media that he quickly became a team spokesman of sorts. "He acted like he'd already been in the big leagues a long time," manager George Bamberger said.

Although Robin arrived in the major leagues three years earlier than Paulie, he is only 11 months older. Both broke into the majors after only a partial season in the minors. Molitor's first game was Opening Day of 1978, and he started at shortstop because Robin was injured. "I remember we were very worried about Robin's absence (at the start of the '78 season)," then-owner Bud Selig recalled before Molitor's Hall of Fame induction in 2004. "George [Bamberger] said to me, 'The kid's going to play shortstop.' I said, 'No, the kid's not going to play' because that was Robin's nickname. George said, 'The other kid. The kid from Minnesota.' I said, 'Oh, really?' Sure enough, Paulie opened the season, and none of us realized how good he was. Within a week or two, Bambi nicknamed him 'The Ignitor,' and he was. Through all the greatness of Cecil Cooper, Ben Oglivie, Gorman Thomas, and the rest, it was always Molitor and Yount."

In Molitor's first full season, he played shortstop, moved to second when Yount came back, and also spent time at third base. He hit .273

with 26 doubles and 30 steals. The following two years, he hit .322 and .304. Then the injury bug bit him...repeatedly. There were groin pulls, hamstring strains, puffy ankles, sprained wrists, dislocated fingers—just about every kind of injury you can imagine. Molitor went on the disabled list in 1980, 1981, 1984, 1985, and twice in 1986 and 1987. The 1984 elbow injury nearly ended his career. Doctors told him he'd likely never be able to throw well enough to play third base again, but he did, though he spent much of his final decade in the majors as a designated hitter.

Some of his former teammates—as well as many opponents of the time—are convinced that injuries cost Molitor a chance to surpass Pete Rose as baseball's all-time hits leader. (He finished with 3,319.) It almost cost him more than that. Molitor developed some well-known personal problems. "A lot about who you end up becoming and the character you develop is how you handle some of the things that maybe you're not so proud of or poor decisions and failures and mistakes," Molitor said at a press conference following his Hall of Fame selection. "It was real and it was problematic and it was something that could have easily cut short my career if I didn't get a grip on it quickly. But you learn from it and find the positive in it and try to use your experiences to help other people. And it makes you appreciate things that are good." On the field Molitor was almost always good. He and Yount, who also transitioned to center field at one point, became $3 million-a-year players but played the game hard, what old-school scouts now refer to as "the right way."

When I played with the Brewers, neither Yount nor Molitor was what you would describe as a "vocal leader." They were just "leaders." When they did say something, it was usually in a helpful way and it had a tremendous impact. The bigger thing, though, was the example they set. They played so hard and so selflessly that they made you want to do the same. It's such a huge benefit when your best players are the hardest-working guys on the club. If you didn't hustle out a ground ball, you felt like you were disrespecting them in a way.

Just about every young player who came across them started out in awe of Paulie and Robin but quickly realized that they were great people as well as great players. If you talk to B.J. Surhoff, Cal Eldred, Bill Wegman, Dale Sveum, Pat Lisatch, Greg Vaughn, and countless others, you'll get the stories. One of my favorites came from former Brewers catcher Mike Matheny, who is now the manager of the St. Louis Cardinals. In spring training in 1992, Matheny was in his first big league camp with the Brewers. Molitor was in his last. Matheny was called up from the low minors for an exhibition game. The Brewers were rallying from a late deficit, but they trailed by enough that manager Phil Garner called Matheny in from the bullpen to hit for Molitor. If Darryl Hamilton reached base, Garner was going to let Molitor hit. If Hamilton made an out, Matheny was going to pinch hit for one of his idols and stay in the game to catch. "I came running down and put on that crazy-looking double ear-flapped helmet, and Molitor walks up and said, 'You look stupid. Put this on,'" Matheny told Rick Hummel of the *St. Louis Post-Dispatch*. "And he gave me his helmet. So I'm standing on deck and, sure enough, Hamilton bloops a double." With all the fans watching, Matheny returned the helmet to Molitor, who stroked a single. "I doubt he remembers that," Matheny said. "We ended up losing, and I went to look at the [lineup] card, and they'd already scratched out Molitor and wrote my name on it. But then they threw it in the trash. I went to grab it, and somebody spit the biggest Red Man spit on it that you'd ever seen. I decided to let it lay. That was my 'almost' moment." Matheny learned his lesson. As a manager he saves the lineup card for players who make their debut or record their first big league hit or strikeout.

Plenty of players—in the Milwaukee, Toronto, and Minnesota organizations—have learned lessons from Molitor. While Robin was regarded by some as the more natural athlete, Paulie was considered the more cerebral player. I don't know if that was fair or accurate because they both were incredible at picking up little things that gave their team an edge. If you gave them a chance, they'd beat you. "I never saw a player, even to this day, that was able to be ready for any situation with two or three alternatives like Molitor," former Brewers manager Tom Trebelhorn told Tracy Ringolsby of the *Rocky Mountain News*. "He was the best guy I ever saw about being ready with 'A' to do, but also maybe 'B' or 'C.' He had the greatest pre-play mode in an era of replay. And he was the greatest base runner I ever saw."

Paulie had that incredibly quick, compact swing. I can't count how many times he would smack the first pitch of the game for a single, steal second, and have us in the lead in the first inning. It was amazing. It also was the guy who always took the extra base or who was able to steal opponents signs quickly. "I remember one time I was struggling at the plate and I told Paulie, 'If you get to second base, you've got to give me the signs so I know what they're going to throw,'" Sal Bando said. "Well, I get to the plate, and he's at second base and he wasn't giving me anything. So I yelled at him in between innings, and he said, 'I don't have them yet.' I said, 'Next time, just guess. I trust your guess more than I trust myself right now.'"

Bando was present for the beginning and end of Molitor's stint in Milwaukee. After selecting Molitor out of the University of Minnesota with the third overall pick in 1977, the Brewers signed him to an $80,000 bonus and brought him to County Stadium for a press conference. After Molitor wore what he called "a big, geeky suit," Bando tossed Yount an outfield glove and told him his days at shortstop were numbered. About 15 years later, in his role as general manager, Bando was on hand for Molitor's exit. The messy divorce took place at the winter meetings in 1992. After a spectacular season under rookie manager Phil Garner, who had the Brewers in contention for a playoff berth until the final weekend of the season, Molitor entered free agency at age 36 with a desire to finish his career in Milwaukee. The Brewers, feeling the crush of small-market economics and fearing injury problems, decided they couldn't afford to keep Molitor, whom Bando regrettably referred to at one point as "just a DH." Toronto swept in with a three-year, $13 million offer. "If Paul Molitor leaving the Brewers doesn't show that the small markets are in trouble, nothing does," Jim Gantner told the *Milwaukee Sentinel* at the time.

Molitor, who wore No 19 in Toronto as an homage to Yount, led the league with 211 hits in 1993 and went on to win a World Series with the Blue Jays, scoring on Joe Carter's dramatic clinching homer and picking up World Series MVP honors. Though he was booed on returns to Milwaukee for several years, many fans were disappointed when, upon leaving Toronto, Molitor chose to play for his hometown Twins rather than return to Milwaukee. Eventually, though, the scars from his Milwaukee departure healed. "When you look back at it, it was just something that was kind of unavoidable," Molitor recalled shortly before his jersey retirement ceremony at County Stadium. "It's the way things were going in the industry at the time with small-market teams losing players. But, it had never happened in Milwaukee. I don't think people knew how to handle it."

As he prepared for his Hall of Fame speech, Molitor reflected on his 15 seasons with the Brewers: "I was lucky to play in Milwaukee at a time when, for the majority of the time, we kept a good core of the players together. Naturally, with Robin, Jimmy [Gantner], and myself, we hold a record for tenure for teammates together. That certainly added to how special my time was in Milwaukee. Because of that it allowed the fans to have more of a personal relationship with the team. County Stadium, while it was one of the older parks in the game, had an atmosphere in the summertime unmatched by at least the majority of other parks. The tailgating and the loyalty of the fans made it a great atmosphere for the players to perform in. The friendship and being there for 15 years and being a part of the community and having a chance to play on a competitive team and in the World Series, all were tremendous highlights of my time in the Brewers organization.

"I certainly was lucky to come into the organization when it was on the rise. The team hadn't won many games prior to 1978, and in my first year, we won 93 games and eventually climbed into the mini-playoffs in 1981 and the World Series in 1982. We regenerated in 1987 and again my last season of 1992 when we came real close to being a playoff team. I was proud of being a part of that. In the end we didn't have the talent that we had in the early '80s, but we had a good group of guys and I was proud that I could go out with a very entertaining, competitive team."

That made the decision to leave all the more difficult. "The longer I played, the more I realized how fortunate I had been to play with one club," Molitor said. "We were at an apex economically in the game. The big market and small-market aspects were prevalent. It was putting players in precarious positions to make decisions of either moving on or staying put. For whatever reason Toronto offered me something that was very attractive. Unfortunately, the Brewers were in a position where they couldn't do a lot. It became apparent to me that it might be time to move. I questioned it for a long time. Later, it was an obvious decision, but my emotions made it difficult because of my attachment to the team, the city, and the fans."

After winning the World Series in '93, Molitor's biggest thrill was getting his 3,000th hit. He accomplished that on September 16, 1996—Yount's birthday—and he did it in Kansas City, where both Robin and George Brett watched his historic triple—unprecedented for a 3,000th hit—from the stands. "I remember getting a base hit in my first at-bat and then I flew out in my second at-bat," Molitor recalled. "I remember hitting the ball high in the air to right-center and I assumed they were going to run it down. Thank God I was taught well to run everything out because all of a sudden the ball falls and I was able to dive into third base with a triple. It hit me right away. A reporter mentioned to me before the game that no one ever hit a triple for their 3,000th hit, so it clicked in my head when I was standing there on third. It was great. [Manager] Tom

Kelly, who rarely comes out of the dugout, all my teammates, mobbed me. It was in Kansas City, and being on the road, the Royals did a nice tribute for me. There's something about that that I truly did appreciate. After all the injuries in my career, I really didn't think it would be possible for me to accomplish that feat. I'm not one to take a lot of credit in this game, but to overcome all those injuries and play long enough to reach that milestone is something I'm most proud of."

Molitor received baseball's ultimate honor in the winter of 2004, when he was selected for the National Baseball Hall of Fame and Museum. He made it on the first ballot, garnering 85 percent of the vote. "I was at home. I had my family and my attorney, Ron Simon, with me," he recalled. "We waited. We knew the call was to come around 12:00. When it came my heart raced, anticipating what was going to be said on the other end of the line. Jack [O'Connell, the secretary of the Baseball Writers Association of America] was very professional and said he was pleased and honored to tell me that I had been elected. There was a huge sigh of relief on my part. The room erupted with some screaming and applause. It was very emotional. I don't think it's one of those moments you can really plan for. You can try to imagine it, but when it happens, it stands on its own merit. We were able to celebrate and raise a glass and have a toast. Naturally, the Hall represents the greatest players in the history of the game. To be accepted the first time I become eligible, makes it even more special. The Hall of Fame isn't something I ever thought or dreamt about when I began playing because of the elite players that are in there. As you play for a long time, things fall into place, and you have longevity and productivity. To be acknowledged in that fashion, well, it's pretty overwhelming."

Asked during induction weekend in Cooperstown, how he'd like to be remembered as a player, Molitor joked that it was an honor to be remembered at all. "I wasn't the type of player that if you came out to one game I was going to overly impress you," he said. "I like the fact that people tell me over a course of time, they can tell that I could make an impact on a team. I tried to be as complete a player as I could. I was all about situational hitting and base running. I looked for little edges. There's something to be said about trying to do things the right way over a long period of time."

MOLITOR'S INDUCTION SPEECH (ABRIDGED)

Cooperstown, New York
July 25, 2004

Thank you, thank you, very much. Mr. Commissioner, honored guests, Hall of Famers, ladies, and gentlemen, and baseball fans everywhere. This truly is a glorious day that the Lord has made. And I'd like to extend my congratulations to Murray and Lon and Dennis. It's an honor to be going in with you guys today. Congratulations to Jane Clark, Dale Petrovskey, Jeff Idelson, Kim Bennett, and the entire staff here at the Hall, I just want to thank you for making these last few months so special for me and my family. And for the Baseball Writers Association of America, you know, what can I say? Thanks for voting for me, and I guess not holding being a DH against me. It's such a privilege to stand before you today. The journey that brought me here to Cooperstown was an amazing one, and I'd like to share some of that with you today.

I grew up in St. Paul, Minnesota, in a wonderful family consisting of my mom and dad, six sisters and a brother. I loved all sports, but baseball was my passion. When that snow would begin to melt and that grass would start to peak through in the spring time, it was time for baseball. My dad and I used to go out in the backyard. And we had the perfect height of a fence for a young aspiring major leaguer to have to leap to his utmost to steal that home run away. And my dad and I could play that game for hours.

I was a huge fan of the Minnesota Twins growing up and I remember listening to all of the games on the radio, waiting to see if my favorite player, Harmon Killebrew, would hit one out. The '65 series against the Dodgers for a nine year old was really something. Drysdale and Sandy pitched it up against guys like Harmon and Tony. You couldn't get much better than that.

I started my Little League days on the fields of Highland Groveland and then went on to Linwood and Oxford playgrounds. I played on a couple of teams per summer and had a game almost every night. I also had a summer job, which was caddying, which was my first job. And I'd always have to ask the caddy master, "I've got to leave early for my games tonight." Finally, he had to offer me the ultimatum, "What do you want to do, make money or play baseball?" I guess I learned later on that you could do both.

As I got older, my passion grew, and my dreams became more vivid. I played ball in school, of course, first at St. Luke's in St. Paul, and then on to Cretin High School, which I know is very well represented here today, a couple hundred in on a charter. I'm grateful to all the coaches that I had growing up who sacrificed their time to help kids like me learn the great game of baseball. But there was one coach who really stood out as being particularly helpful and influencing both for me as a ballplayer and as a young man, and his name is Bill Peterson. I played for Bill for almost six years. He was my coach for VFW, American Legion, high school. And he just had a way with our clubs. Our practices were always full of energy and lots of chatter, people running all over the place. Any time we had a bad practice meant lining up and doing headfirst slides. But those were the exceptions because Bill had a way of bringing out the best of all of us every day. Bill just also happened to have coached Dave Winfield. Not bad. Two kids from St. Paul finding their way to Cooperstown, and both come through Bill Peterson's program. So thanks for everything, Billy P.

It was onto the University of Minnesota to play for Dick Siebert and George Thomas. I'm indebted to the university for giving me the chance to continue my education as well as play for a legendary college coach who we fondly refer to as "the Chief." Dick was a stickler for fundamentals, and when you practice indoors for two months in the winter time, you get pretty good at them. One of the reasons I think I got to the majors so quickly was that because of Dick's program, I was fundamentally sound, as Dan Patrick would say. And I know Chief was the one who helped me get that way. During my time at Minnesota, I played for a man named Sam Suplizio. And even though my summer was cut short when I broke my jaw, Sam and I became good friends and remain that way today. I appreciate you, Sammy.

I was drafted by the Brewers after my junior year. A couple of scouts, Tony Siegel and Dee Fondy, thought I was worthy of a first-round selection. I went on to Burlington, Iowa, to play for the Bees under Denis Menke. And it was a great summer in Burlington, winning down there. And Denis helped me realize if I was ever going to get to the majors, I was never going to be a power hitter, so I canned that idea and started to try to learn to hit the ball to all fields.

It was on to my first major league camp in '78. You know, I survived some pretty ugly days early in camp, as most rookies have. There was even one day when Frank Howard asked me if the scout was drunk when he signed me. But somehow I made the Opening Day roster, largely due in part to an injury to Robin, and it was the beginning of a very memorable 15 years in Milwaukee. Yes, it was.

Harry Dalton and the organization put together quite an amazing team back then and we had quite a cast of characters. But when you put us all the together we could really play. We knew how to have fun and we knew how to win. In 1982 we waited until the last day of the season to win the division, and then, of course, falling behind the Angels 0–2 before coming back, and the Brewers finally had themselves first World Series. I'll always remember late in Game 5 of the playoffs, Cecil Cooper, a big hit. He drove in Jimmy Gantner and Charlie Moore. And an inning later, Rodney hit a ball to Robin at short and he threw over to Cecil, and County Stadium just went ballistic. I think it was the loudest I ever heard that place. And I think Ozzie probably remembers that one, wherever Ozzie is.

I'd like to thank Commissioner Selig for his leadership and friendship while he owned the Brewers. Bud was a great one to play for and he was a true fan of the game. His door was always open, and I often took advantage. We had some great talks about a lot of different things or, as Bud would say, "a plethora of things." I learned a great deal from Mr. Selig. One of the best parts about my time in Milwaukee—and I see both of their jerseys over there— was playing with Robin Yount and Jimmy Gantner the entire time I was there. In fact, we set the record for longest teammates, for 15 years. Jimmy was what I would call an overachiever, and that's not a knock. He wasn't really picked to be a major league player, but he put together an incredible 17-year career.

And I've just got to share a couple of Jimmy stories. Jimmy had a way with the English language that would make Yogi proud. I'll give you a couple of examples. There's a time Jimmy got in a rundown, and somehow he found a way to make contact with the infielder and he looked at the umpire and he started yelling, "That's construction, that's construction." And I remember being in a clinic with him one time for kids, and Jimmy was talking about hitting and the importance of balance. He was talking about, "you've got to make sure you stay on the palms of your feet. That will keep you locked in." Those are just a couple of Gumby-isms for you.

What can I say about Robin? I learned so much from Robin. Although we were contemporaries in age, he had played in the big leagues for four years before I got there. Robin had a simple philosophy about playing: "What can I do to help my team win today?" And believe me, there was a lot of things that Robin Yount could do to help his team win. I'm honored to follow him into the Hall as the second player to wear a Brewers hat on his plaque.

Well, the fans of Milwaukee, Wisconsin, were always tremendously supportive. There were so many days when I arrived to County Stadium, and there would already be 10 to 15,000 people in the parking lot, five hours before game time. I think it's pretty obvious they invented tailgating. And I'll always remember the parade that you put on for us in 1982, even though we lost. I always told people, judging by the reaction of the crowd that day, you would never have been able to tell, did we win or did we lose, that's how supported we felt as players. So, thank you, Milwaukee fans, for making my time there so special.

It was on to Toronto in '93. And I want to thank Paul Beeston and Pat Gillick for bringing me in to try to help the Blue Jays defend their title of '92. Defend it we did. And it had been 11 years since I had been into a World Series, and I was determined to savor every moment. And then there was the moment with Joe Carter's home run, I was finally able to enter the winner's circle. I'm indebted to the Jays' organization for the opportunity and I would like to thank them along with the Blue Jay fans who showed up 4 million strong in '93 for giving me three great years in the beautiful city of Toronto.

It was time to go back home, complete the circle. Terry Ryan brought me back to Minnesota to play for the team that I followed as a kid. My friends and family could hop in the car and drive down to the Metrodome just like the old days on the playground. You know, I remember the fans giving me a standing ovation my first at-bat back in the Metrodome and I also remember promptly honoring it by striking out. But I had three very enjoyable years in Minnesota playing for Tom Kelly, who I learned a great deal from. And once again I was able to follow Dave Winfield's path and I got my 3,000th hit back at home playing for the Twins, and remarkably, we did it on the exact same day. So Dave and my career had a lot of parallels. The only downside going back to Minnesota, other than not winning enough games, was I hoped to have a chance to play with Kirby Puckett, and we all know Puck had to retire with glaucoma, and it would have been great. But Puck, I'm happy to be on your team now. So, appreciate you, brother...

I look behind me and I see a group of incredible men. Some of these men are the gentlemen that helped fuel my passion as a youngster. And then there are other men that I had a chance to either compete with, compete against, or play with. And, of course, there are the other Hall of Famers who aren't able to be here today. Together they compile an amazing fraternity of baseball brothers that parallel the history of this great game. And I want to thank them all for making me feel so welcome and embracing me into the family of the Hall of Fame. And all the fans that came out today, I appreciate you more than you know sharing in this day with me.

Thank you, everybody, and God bless you.

Bob Uecker

Bob Uecker never played an inning for the Brewers. He never hit a homer, never struck out, grounded into a double play, or was charged with a passed ball. But he will always be one of the most important figures in franchise history. Brewers fans know that he is a Wisconsin treasure. They've welcomed him into their homes, cars, backyard barbecues, fishing boats, and lakeside cabins for decades. "The wit and wisdom of Bob Uecker is part of our community's collective psyche," Brewers owner Mark Attanasio said a few years ago.

I admire Bob Uecker for a lot of reasons, and it's not just because he was a regular guest (and one of Johnny Carson's favorites) on *The Tonight Show* or because he starred in *Major League* and *Mr. Belvedere* or on *Saturday Night Live*. All of those things were awesome, and Uecker was fantastic in them. But what I admire most about Bob is the way he shows up at the ballpark every day and is on top of his game. I learned so much from Bob, watching him go about his business. Every day, he comes to the park and he is invigorated to do the game. When you talk to him, you can never tell if the team is bad, good, or indifferent.

Watching him, I learned that you take the broadcasting job one day at a time. You don't worry that the team is 20 games out. First place? Last place? It doesn't matter. You just hope for a good game that day. You don't rip people. Bob has a good attitude and he clearly enjoys what he's doing. I guarantee that the reason he gets out of bed in the morning every day is to come to the ballpark. There is no question about that. When he gets to the park at 3:30 every afternoon, you see it. He loves talking to the guys. He loves hanging around batting practice. He has to love it to put up with all the flights and hotels and all the headaches that the job can bring. Nothing outweighs his love for baseball. It's a special thing that he has in him that has kept him going through all the years of travel and all his surgeries and family things. Baseball is his life. It's his touchstone. Brewers fans are lucky to have him. He's had a lot of opportunities to do other things, but he's always put Milwaukee and Wisconsin first.

It's almost impossible to hang around Ueck and not laugh. He's one of the funniest people on the planet. The stories he tells are legendary, and you seldom hear the same one twice. In April of 2014, the Brewers had a ceremony—his second such honor—to dedicate a statue to Ueck. He has the statue out in front of Miller Park. But the second one was a figure of him seated in the "front row," which is actually the top of the upper deck—behind a pole—near Section 422. There is an empty seat next to the statue, which allows fans to take a picture next to "Ueck" in exchange for a monetary donation to the Brewers Community Foundation and the Make-A-Wish Foundation. "It's going to be a fun thing for fans and a way to generate money for the charities," Uecker said at the dedication ceremony. "Fans will be able to go up there and sit next to me, maybe a lap dance."

To me, the highlight of the dedication ceremony that day came when Robin Yount stepped to the microphone. Yount, who was an 18-year-old shortstop when he met Uecker, and is one of Bob's closest friends, noticed immediately that the event was held in the afternoon with only a

The always entertaining and engaging Bob Uecker announces a Brewers game during July of 2003.

smattering of media members on hand. "God, this unbelievable," Yount said. "Fifty thousand empty seats. What a ceremony."

When the laughter died down, Yount launched into a Uecker story that I had never heard. It also speaks to Uecker's ability to get everyone to join in on the fun: "We were in Detroit. We had a day game. After the game six or eight of us went to a restaurant. We were there a while. And after that...the hotel was about four or five blocks away. Now Detroit back in those days kind of shut down at night, so there wasn't nearly as much traffic downtown as there was earlier. When dinner was over, it was time to leave. For whatever reason, Ueck decided to march us back to the hotel. Like a Marine sergeant, he called cadence, told all of us to line up, and we would march back. So we do that. From the sidewalk we get out to the middle of this four-lane highway, right down the center. Not a lot of traffic at the time. But there were a few cars. And he's calling cadence, okay. This is fun.

"A cop car pulls up, asks Ueck what we were doing. Ueck says to the policeman, 'We're marching. What's it look like we're doing?' [The] police officer says, 'Okay,' pulls his car over to the curb. [Ueck asks] 'What are you guys doin'?' They don't really respond, and Ueck tells them to get in line. And, they do—one cop at the front of the line, the other at the rear. We march roughly two or three blocks from that point, led by police officers, to the hotel. We get to the hotel, and it has revolving doors. One police officer gets on one side of the revolving door, and the other on the other side. As everyone of us walks through that revolving door, they salute us and say 'Good luck tomorrow.' That's the type of person Bob Uecker is. I'm not sure what type that is. He didn't get thrown in jail. None of us got thrown in jail. We had a lot of fun and so did the police officers."

Ueck was born in Milwaukee on January 26, 1934. His father, August, immigrated from Switzerland and worked as mechanic and in a tool and die shop. His mother, Mary, was born in Michigan. Uecker grew up on the north side of Milwaukee, around 10th Street and Meinecke Avenue, which was close to Borchert Field, then home of the Milwaukee Brewers of the American Association. "We were up there all the time as kids," Uecker said. "After the fifth inning, they'd let you in for nothing. Most of the time, we'd just climb over the fence. We knew how to get in."

He wasn't just a spectator. Although he's made a career out of belittling his ability, Uecker was a tremendous athlete. A standout on the sandlot and at Milwaukee Boys Tech High School, he started out as a pitcher but changed course after working out for Braves pitching coach Jonny Cooney at County Stadium. "I was throwing for about 15 minutes," Uecker said. "I thought I was doing pretty good, but Cooney said, 'Alright, now let me see your good fastball.' I said, 'I've been throwing my good fastball.' And, he told me—this is no joke—'Well, then I recommend you get a job.'"

After a stint in the army, where he spent time playing baseball with a special service unit that included future big league shortstop Dick Groat, Uecker returned home and signed with his hometown Milwaukee Braves for $3,000.

"That bothered my dad at the time because he didn't have that kind of dough," Uecker has facetiously said the line countless times at banquets and nightclubs and on late-night TV couches. "But eventually, he scraped it up."

Uecker excelled in the minor leagues. He hit 19 homers in his first pro season and batted .310 with 22 homers and 81 RBIs in Double A. He made it to the major leagues in an era when there were just 16 teams. He played for the Braves, St. Louis Cardinals, and Philadelphia Phillies. He was a backup on the Cardinals' 1964 World Series championship team. He hit .200 with 14 homers in his career, but four of them were off Hall of Fame pitchers: Sandy Koufax (twice), Fergie Jenkins, and Gaylord Perry. "Every time I see Gaylord, he says, 'Here comes the worst day of my life,'" Uecker said upon winning the Ford C. Frick Award in 2003. "Every time I see Sandy Koufax, I apologize. I always thought I was going to keep him out of the Hall of Fame."

Uecker's most memorable moment, other than leading the league in passed balls in 1967, may have come during the 1964 World Series. "We were taking batting practice," recalled Tim McCarver, who was the starting catcher for the Cardinals and went on to be a broadcaster. "Ueck's job was protect Bob Kuban, and the band that was playing in left field. They took a break. Roger Craig said, 'Ueck, why don't you grab a tuba?' He dropped his glove, grabbed the tuba, and caught about five balls in it. I remember [Cardinals general manager] Bob Howsam sent him a bill for $116 after the World Series for damage to the tuba. It was one of the funniest things I've ever seen. The two guys who enjoyed it most were Mickey Mantle and Roger Maris. They'd never seen anything like it."

Uecker recalls the incident, which was captured in photos. "I was better with the tuba than I was with a glove," he said. The jokes about his career flow easily, but Uecker is proud of his time as a player and the respect that he has earned from players of his era and today. "I did play in the big leagues," he said. "I made jokes because it made people laugh. Who is going to brag about what I did in my career? Nobody. I just joked about it to have fun."

His jokes are legendary. Here are some of my favorites:

- "The way to catch a knuckleball is to wait until it stops rolling and then pick it up."
- "When I looked at the third-base coach for a sign, he turned his back on me."
- "I knew when my career was over. In 1965 my baseball card came out with no picture."
- "People have asked me a lot of times because I didn't hit a lot—we all know that—how long a dozen bats would last me. Depending on the weight and the model that I was using at that particular time, I would say about eight to 10 cookouts."
- "I ordered a dozen bats, and they came back with handles at each end."
- "I had been playing for a while and I asked Louisville Slugger to send me a dozen flame-treated bats. When I got it, I saw it was a box of ashes."
- "I helped the Cardinals win the pennant in '64. I came down with hepatitis. The trainer injected me with it."
- "The highlight of my career? In '67 with St. Louis, I walked with the bases loaded to drive in the winning run in an intrasquad game in spring training."

- "Actually, I had two career highlights: I got an intentional walk from Sandy Koufax and I got out of a rundown against the Mets."
- "I once hit a grand slam off Ron Herbel, and when his manager, Herman Franks, came out to get him, he brought Herbel's suitcase."
- "I didn't get a lot of awards as a player, but they did have a 'Bob Uecker Day Off' for me once in Philly."
- "When I came up to bat with three men on and two out in the ninth inning, I looked in the other team's dugout, and they were already in street clothes."
- "They said I was such a great prospect that they were sending me to a winter league to sharpen up. When I stepped off the plane, I was in Greenland."
- "Sporting companies used to pay me really good money not to be seen using their products."
- "The manager came up to me before a game and told me they don't allow visitors in the clubhouse."
- "I led the league in, 'Go get 'em next time.'"
- "I think my top salary was maybe in 1966. I made $17,000 and I think 11 grand of that came from selling other players' equipment."
- "If a guy hits .300 every year, what does he have to look forward to? I always tried to stay around .190 with three or four RBIs. And I tried to get them all in September. That way I always had something to talk about during the winter."
- "In 1962 I was named Minor League Player of the Year. It was my second season in the bigs."
- "The biggest thrill a ballplayer can have is when your son takes after you. That happened when my Bobby was in his championship Little League game. He really showed me something, struck out three times, made an error that lost the game. Parents were throwing things at our car and swearing at us as we drove off. Gosh, I was proud."

- "I had slumps that lasted into the winter."
- "Anybody with ability can play in the big leagues. But to be able to trick people year in and year out the way I did I think that was a much greater feat."

When his playing career ended, Uecker found a way to remain in base-ball—and in Milwaukee. Brewers owner Bud Selig, who had been a friend to many Braves players, including Uecker over the years, offered him a job as a scout. The result of that assignment has become legend. "We sent him up to the Northern League, and the next thing I know [GM] Frank Lane comes raging into my office, asking what kind of scout I'd hired," Selig recalls. "I wasn't sure what he meant, and then he threw down Bob's scout-ing report. It was covered with mashed potatoes and gravy. You couldn't read it. Lane said he was the worst scout in baseball history. So, we decided to put him in the booth."

The story has been told countless times, and Uecker doesn't refute it. "Frank Lane called me and told me he wants me to go up and scout the Northern League," Uecker said. "I had never scouted. I went to Aberdeen, Fargo, and Sioux Falls. I don't have anything, not a stop-watch, nothing. I had to come back to the room and make out scout-ing reports in triplicate. I go with this scout in Fargo to the American Legion Post, where all the scouts ate dinner. I took a stack of reports with me and I had mashed potatoes, gravy, and beef. As I'm writing on the table, some of it falls on the reports. I don't want to do them over, so I just wiped it off and I put it in a batch I sent back. Frank Lane goes into Bud's office and throws these things on his desk and says, 'What the hell is this?' On the bottom of every report, I put 'FML.' Fringe major leaguer. Just in case he made it."

Uecker went into the booth in 1971, working with Merle Harmon and Tom Collins. "Those guys helped me a lot," Uecker said. "I had never done any broadcasting—other than talking into a beer cup in the bullpen and trying to make the other guys out there laugh. I don't care who you are. When you get up in the booth, it's totally different than it is down on the field. It's a learning process. You've never done it before. You might have been interviewed or talked in front of a camera. But that's totally different from sitting in front of a microphone and telling people what is happening. You've got to find a comfort zone real quick. The more and more you do it, the more comfortable you get. I don't think there's any gig that I ever did that I wasn't nervous. Not afraid, but nervous about being up to it. The first *Tonight Show* I ever did, I was standing backstage and I thought, *Holy Jesus! What did I get myself into?* You go out, and there are millions of people watching. You've got to find that comfort zone."

He looked totally at ease talking to Johnny Carson, hosting *Saturday Night Live*, starring in *Mr. Belvedere*, and bringing humor to the classic Miller Lite "Tastes Great! Less Filling" spots, but Uecker's comfort zone is the ballpark—especially Miller Park. He may like the golf course or fishing on his boat, but he is happiest when he's hanging out, talking to old friends in the dugout, the batting cage, and the press box. "I was born and raised in Milwaukee," he said. "I never wanted to go anywhere else. I had opportunities. I don't consider this a job anyway to be able to do a game each and every day throughout the summer and talk to people. Every night at 6:30, you become part of people's families. That's part of the reward. To be recognized by the way you talk, the way you describe a game. That's one of the big rewards of doing this job."

UECKER'S FORD C. FRICK AWARD ACCEPTANCE SPEECH

Cooperstown, New York
July 27, 2003

Thank you, Joe, thank you very much. And thank you, ladies and gentlemen. And my congratulations to Hal, Gary Carter, Eddie Murray, and to all of the members of the staff of the Hall of Fame, thank you very much. This has been a wonderful, wonderful time.

I, in deference to Hal McCoy, was asked to quit many times. I was born and raised in Milwaukee, Wisconsin. Actually, I was born in Illinois. My mother and father were on an oleo margarine run to Chicago back in 1934 because we couldn't get colored margarine in Wisconsin. On the way home, my mother was with child—me. And the pains started, and my dad pulled off into an exit area, and that's where the event took place. I remember it was a nativity type setting. An exit light shining down. There were three truck drivers there. One guy was carrying butter, one guy had frankfurters, and the other guy was a retired baseball scout who told my folks that I probably had a chance to play somewhere down the line.

I remember it being very cold. It was January. I didn't weigh very much. I think the birth certificate said something like 10 ounces. I was very small. And I remember the coldness on my back from the asphalt. And I was immediately wrapped in swaddling clothes and put in the back of a '37 Chevy without a heater. And that was the start of this Cinderella story that you are hearing today.

I did not have a lot of ability as a kid, and my dad wanted me to have everything that everybody else had. I think the first thing that he ever bought me was a football. And I was very young. He didn't know a lot about it. He came from the old country. I mean, we tried to pass it and throw it and kick it and we couldn't do it. And it was very discouraging for him and for me. Almost, we almost quit. And finally we had a nice enough neighbor. [He] came over and put some air in it and what a difference.

I got a lot of my ability from my father. As a lot of these other guys did, my father actually came to this country as a soccer player. He didn't play. He blew up the balls is what he did. And they didn't have pumps in those days. And to see a man put that valve in his mouth and insert it into a soccer ball and blow thirty pounds of air and then have the ability to pull that thing out without it fracturing the back of his mouth was unbelievable. You had to see his neck and his veins popping. It was unbelievable. How proud I was as I watched him do it time after time.

My first sport was eighth grade basketball. And my dad didn't want to buy me the supporter Johnny, you know, to do the job. So my mother made me one out of a flour sack. And the tough thing about that is, you put that thing on, you whip it out of your bag in the gym. You know all the guys are looking at it. And you start the game. The guy guarding you knows exactly where you're going since little specks of flour keep dropping out. And then right down the front it says "Pillsbury's Best."

I signed a very modest $3,000 bonus with the Braves in Milwaukee, which I'm sure a lot of you know. And my old man didn't have that kind of money to put out. But the Braves took it. I remember sitting around our kitchen table counting all this money, coins out of jars, and I'm telling my dad, "Forget this, I don't want to play." He said, "No, you are going to play baseball. We are going to have you make some money, and we're going to live real good." My dad had an accent. I want to be real authentic when I'm doing this thing. So I signed. The signing took place at a very popular restaurant in Milwaukee. And I remember driving, and my dad's all fired up and nervous, and I said, "Look, it will be over in a couple of minutes. Don't be uptight." We pull in the parking lot, pull next to the Braves automobile, and my dad screwed up right away. He doesn't have the window rolled up far enough, and our tray falls off, and all the food is on the floor. And from there on it was baseball.

Starting with the Braves in Milwaukee, St. Louis, where I won the world championship for them in 1964, to the Philadelphia Phillies and back to the Braves in Atlanta where I became Phil Niekro's personal chaser. But during every player's career there comes a time when you know that your services are no longer required, that you might be moving on—traded, sold, released, whatever it may be. And having been with four clubs, I picked up a few of these tips. I remember Gene Mauch doing things to me at Philadelphia. I'd be sitting there and he'd say, "Grab a bat and stop this rally." [He'd] send me up there without a bat and tell me to try for a walk, look down at the first-base coach for a sign, and have him turn his back on you.

But you know what? Things like that never bothered me. I'd set records that will never be equaled, 90 percent I hope are never printed: .200 lifetime batting average in the major leagues, which tied me with another sports great averaging .200 or better for a 10-year period, Don Carter, one of our top bowlers. In 1967 I set a major league record for passed balls and I did that without playing every game. There was a game, as a matter of fact, during that year when Phil Niekro's brother and me were pitching against each other in Atlanta. Their parents were sitting right behind home plate. I saw their folks that day more than they did the whole weekend.

But with people like Niekro, and this was another thing, I found the easy way out to catch a knuckleball. It was to wait until it stopped rolling and then pick it up. There were a lot of things that aggravated me, too. My family is here today—my boys, my girls. My kids used to do things that aggravate me, too. I'd take them to the game, and they'd want to come home with a different player. I remember one of my friends came to Atlanta to see me once. He came to the door, he says, "Does Bob Uecker live here?" He says, "Yeah, bring him in." But my two boys are just like me. In their championship Little League game, one of them struck out three times, and the other one had an error, allowing the winning run to score. They lost the championship, and I couldn't have been more proud. I remember the people as we walked through the parking lot throwing eggs and rotten stuff at our car. What a beautiful day.

You know, everybody remembers their first game in the major leagues. For me it was in Milwaukee. My hometown, born and raised there, and I can remember walking out on the field, and Birdie Tebbetts was our manager at that time. And my family was there: my mother and dad and all my relatives. And as I'm standing on the field, everybody's pointing at me and waving and laughing and I'm pointing back. And Birdie Tebbetts came up and asked me if I was nervous or uptight about the game. And I said, "I'm not. I've been waiting five years to get here. I'm ready to go."

He said, "Well, we're gonna start you today. I didn't want to tell you earlier. I didn't want you to get too fired up."

I said, "Look, I'm ready to go."

He said, "Well, great, you're in there. And oh, by the by, the rest of us up here wear that supporter on the inside." That was the first game my folks walked out on, too.

But you know, of all of the things that I've done, this has always been No. 1, baseball. The commercials, the films, the television series, I could never wait for everything to get over to get back to baseball. I still, and this is not sour grapes by any means, still think I should have gone in as a player. Thank you very much.

The proof is in the pudding. No, this conglomeration of greats that are here today, a lot of them were teammates, but they won't admit it. But they were. And a lot of them were players that worked in games that I called. They are wonderful friends and always will be. And the 1964 World Championship team, the great Lou Brock. And I remember as we got down near World Series time, Bing Devine, who was the Cardinals' general manager at that time, asked me if I would do him and the Cardinals, in general, a favor. And I said I would. And he said, "We'd like to inject you with hepatitis. We need to bring an infielder up." I said, "Would I be able to sit on the bench." He said, "Yes, we'll build a plastic cubicle for you because it is an infectious disease." And I've got to tell you this. I have a photo at home, I turned a beautiful color yellow and with that Cardinal white uniform. I was knocked out. It was beautiful, wasn't it, Lou? It was great.

Of course, any championship involves a World Series [ring]. The ring, the ceremony, the following season in St. Louis at old Busch Stadium. We were standing along the sideline. I was in the bullpen warming up the pitcher. And when they called my name for the ring, it's something that you never ever forget. And when they threw it out into left field, I found it in the fifth inning, I think it was, Lou, wasn't it? And once I spotted it in the grass man, I was on it. It was unbelievable.

But as these players have bats, gloves, I had a great shoe contract and glove contract with a company who paid me a lot of money never to be seen using their stuff. Bat orders—I would order a dozen bats, and there were times they'd come back with handles at each end. You know, people have asked me a lot of times because I didn't hit a lot—we all know that—how long a dozen bats would last me? Depending on the weight and the model that I was using at that particular time, I would say eight to 10 cookouts.

I once ordered a dozen flame-treated bats, and they sent me a box of ashes, so I knew at that time things were moving on. But there are tips that you pick up when the Braves were going to release me. It is a tough time for a manager, for your family, for the player to be told that you're never going to play the game again. And I can remember walking in the clubhouse that day, and Luman Harris, who was the Braves' manager, came up to me and said there were no visitors allowed. So again, I knew I might be moving on.

Paul Richards was the general manager and told me the Braves wanted to make me a coach for the following season and that

I would be coaching second base. So again, gone. But that's when the baseball career started as a broadcaster. I remember working first with Milo Hamilton and Ernie Johnson. And I was all fired up about that, too, until I found out that my portion of the broadcast was being used to jam Radio Free Europe. And I picked up a microphone one day, and my mic had no cord on it, so I was talking to nobody. But it's such a wonderful, wonderful thing today to be here. And one of my first partners was mentioned earlier, Merle Harmon, and Tom Collins, he's here today. All of those who I have worked with from Merle to Lorn Brown to Dwayne Mosley, Pat Hughes, who now works for the Chicago Cubs, and my current partner today, Jim Powell, and Kent Summerfeld. My thanks to all of you.

To my good pal, Bob Costas, out there. Thank you, Bobby. All of the network people, that has been as much a part of broadcasting for me as anything. The days with ABC and Monday Night Baseball with the late Bob Prince and Keith Jackson and Al Michaels and my great pal, Don Drysdale. All of those people have played such a big part in me being here today. Dick Ebersol, the head of NBC Sports. All of them are a big part of what I am. My family is seated over here. I love them very much.

Ulice Payne is here, the president of the Brewers. The commissioner of baseball is a guy that gave me my start. He said, "I want to bring you back to Milwaukee." And I said, "I'll come." And here I am, 33 years later. Thank you, Al. I call him Al, Bud Selig. Wife Sue is here. To all of my Brewer family, Wendy, Laurel Selig, Wendy Selig-Prieb, Laurel Prieb. Tony Migliaccio, one of my great friends. Mike LaBoe, all my people. Jon Greenberg, I didn't even know you were here. You took care of Hal McCoy. What the hell's going on? But all of these people play such a big part in all of our lives.

And to all of you baseball fans around America and any place else, for your letters, your thoughts, your kindness for all of these years, it's been a great run, but No. 1 has always been baseball for me. No matter what else I ever did, baseball was the only way I wanted to go. I thank you very much for your attention today, thank you for having me and congratulations to everybody here. Thank you very much, everybody, thank you.

PART II:
SMORGASBORD OF STORIES

Food

Because I grew up near Philadelphia, a lot of Brewers fans, who visit "The City of Brotherly Love" to catch a series at Citizens Bank Park, ask me the classic question: Pat's or Geno's? They're talking, of course, about Philly cheesesteaks. The signature sandwich, made on a hoagie roll features thinly sliced pieces of ribeye steak, provolone, American, or Cheez Whiz (depending on your preference), along with sautéed onions, mushrooms, and peppers.

Cheesesteaks are to Philly what bratwurst is to Milwaukee. They are a source of civic pride and constant debate. Pat's and Geno's, which have outlets near the stadium complex, are the most popular purveyors. Just like Wisconsin has several bratwurst manufacturers—Klement's is my personal favorite, but Usinger's and Johnsonville are great, too—Philly has multiple cheesesteak outlets, and folks argue about which is best. When people ask my opinion, I generally go the politically correct route. My favorite cheesesteak is the one on my plate! For me cheesesteaks are a once-a-year indulgence.

For Brewers bullpen catcher Marcus Hanel, they are a bit of an obsession. Hanel, who is beginning his 17th year in his role as bullpen catcher, batting practice pitcher, and general assignment coach, made national news in the summer of 2015 when he broke the Citizens Bank Park record for cheesesteaks consumed by a visitor during a four-game series. The cheesesteaks in the Citizens Bank Park clubhouse don't come from an outside source. They're prepared by the visiting clubhouse staff—Mike Chernow, Brian Parks, and Mike Garuccio—who keep precise records of consumption.

Former Brewers right fielder Corey Hart held the single-day record for active players with seven. When the Brewers got to town in 2015, the record for a three-game series was 18 sandwiches set by Hanel's counterpart with the New York Mets, bullpen catcher Eric Langill. Miami Marlins right-hander Mat Latos held the four-day record with 18.

Hanel, who stands 6'5" and weighs 270 pounds and is known by the nickname "Koos," derived from "Marcus," cruised past both of them. By the time the fourth game of the series had even started, he had downed 20. He ended up at 23. "It's just a fun little thing that we do in Philly," Hanel said. "It's one of the things you look forward to on a road trip. [Brewers third-base coach] Ed Sedar said something to me about breaking the record. There was a little prodding." Though he didn't weigh himself before and after his cheesesteak binge, Hanel did say he was "ready to move on" when the Brewers left Philadelphia (after a four-game sweep). "I was a little sluggish and my stomach was a little hard, but I felt okay," he said.

Hanel, who grew up in Racine, Wisconsin, which is roughly 30 miles south of Miller Park, is known for his gigantic hands. He can hold seven baseballs in one hand, which earned him a secondary nickname, "Hooks." In 2005 Hanel started a charity "Koos for Kids," which hosts events and raises money for underprivileged and special-needs children. Hanel is such a popular figure in the clubhouse that many Brewers players attend his events as a way to pay him back for all the batting practice he throws, bullpen sessions, and extra work that he puts in for them. "He's just a great dude," All-Star catcher Jonathan Lucroy said.

It's easy to get spoiled in the big leagues, where the travel is first-class and the food is always great—and in copious amounts, as evidenced by Hanel's eating display—and they give you $100.50 a day for meals and incidental expenses.

The minor leagues, though, are a different story. When I was in El Paso, Texas, the owner had a deal with an airline. I forget which one it was, and it probably doesn't exist anymore. We would fly to all the cities that were close by—Amarillo, Midland, and places like that because we had a deal with a charter company for a short trip. But we actually had to travel by bus on the longer trips—to Jackson, Mississippi, and Tulsa, Oklahoma, etc.

In 1981 our meal money was $12 a day. That wasn't a lot of money even back then. There are only so many Denny's Grand Slam breakfasts that you can consume in a condensed period of time. My buddy, Doug Loman, an outfielder who went on to have a cup of coffee with the Brewers, and I were sick of eating at places like the Waffle House and Denny's, so we got a brilliant idea.

During a trip to Tulsa, we found a supermarket and bought a loaf of bread and a big tube of liver sausage. For three days that was all we ate. We might have had some catsup, too, but we ate liverwurst sandwiches for every meal. We thought we were being so smart with our money and getting great value. Now if you've ever consumed a lot of liverwurst, you have an idea what effect it has on the body. Needless to say, we weren't very popular guys on the team bus. It was pretty bad. And I'm pretty sure a couple of the home-plate umpires were upset with my flatulence, too. I couldn't help it. To this day I am not able to eat liver sausage. I had a similar experience with Southern Comfort, but that's a story for another time.

BILL'S FAVORITE NL CENTRAL RESTAURANTS

We spend a lot of time on the road during the season and, thanks to the schedule, much of it is spent in the cities of our National League Central Division rivals. Here are a handful of my favorite dining spots in the division.

Cincinnati

I love Izzy's Deli. It was established in 1901 and has been a fixture in Cincinnati with several locations. I go to the downtown spot. Their slogan, "World's Greatest Reubens," may generate debate in some circles, but you won't get an argument from me. I always get the turkey reuben, and every sandwich comes with a potato pancake prepared to perfection. I could eat there every day. Cincinnati is also proud of its chili. I used to hit Skyline Chili every trip. It's good, but as I've aged, my body just doesn't process the "five-way"—a mountain of spaghetti, chili, cheese, beans, and onions—like it used to. At night I like to go to Jeff Ruby's steakhouse downtown. It's a spot I frequent with the coaches and Bob Uecker and Tony Migliaccio and his staff. The steaks are great, and the side dishes are fantastic. I love the Montgomery Inn's ribs, too.

Chicago

There are so many great restaurants in Chicago that it's hard to go wrong. Day games at Wrigley give you a chance to try different places. I'm a creature of habit, though. If I get up early, I'll go to the Original Pancake House, which is located down off of State Street. A couple times a season, you'll find me at Geno's East for deep dish pizza. I also like to hit Mike Ditka's restaurant for lunch or dinner. There are plenty of TVs, which make it a great place to watch a game.

Pittsburgh

I look forward to every series in Pittsburgh because I can get breakfast at one of my all-time favorite "greasy spoon" diners in the square: Cherries Diner. I grew up in Jersey, so I know my way around a diner. At Cherries you can get two eggs, bacon, and toast for $5. It's good, too, you'll find me there almost every morning for breakfast. Pittsburgh is famous for Primanti Bros. sandwiches, which are deliciously piled with meat, cole slaw, and French fries, but I can't handle those as well these days as in the past. At night for dinner when we have a chance, I like to go to The Pleasure Bar & Restaurant in Bloomfield, the Little Italy section of town. It is some of the best Italian food I've ever had. The gravy (or sauce) is incredible. I like to get the stuffed shells. The pizza bread is really good, too. I discovered that place on the recommendation of former Brewers skipper Ken Macha, who grew up in Pittsburgh. I owe Ken for that one. It's one of my favorites.

St. Louis

This is another city known for Italian food. There are a number of great restaurants near "the Hill," which is near where Yogi Berra and Joe Garagiola were raised. When we have a day game or a day off, I try to hit Charlie Gitto's, which serves an amazing house salad and chicken parmiagiana, which is fantastic. My favorite spot, though, in St. Louis is Bogart's Smokehouse, a barbecue joint located a short cab ride from the ballpark. I love the combo meal with pulled pork and burnt ends, along with grilled corn and beans. It's one of my favorites. I also try to hit Mike Shannon's, a steakhouse named for the Cardinals' legendary broadcaster. You can always get a great steak, cold beer, and great baseball conversation at Shannon's.

Team Parties

When your team is out of contention in the waning days of September, there isn't much to look forward to other than the rookie dress-up day and the team party. I don't know what it's like now, but we used to have some awesome team parties. In most cases a veteran player would organize the affair, which usually took place at a bar or restaurant. It was always on the road and usually took place on a day off.

At times, the revelry could get a bit out of hand. One year in Boston, several players stayed out very late, and I'll protect the identity of the guilty parties by not naming names. The next night was cold and drizzly and foggy. We were facing one of Boston's best pitchers, and one our best players was hung over. The player in question, who wasn't even sure if he was going to be able to play that day, stepped in for an at-bat and waved feebly at two fastballs. Down in the count 0–2, he hit a hanging curveball for a base hit. He ended up coming around to score and, looking green around the gills, said to no one in particular: "How come pitchers are so stupid? I couldn't touch the fastball and he throws me a curve?"

After that inning the player in question was warming up in the field and had to take a knee. From the stands it may have looked like he was tying his shoe. In reality he was vomiting on the grass. As you can imagine, the team party was deemed a success.

Another year, the team party was held in Baltimore. It was upstairs at a popular bar. It started out as a players-only thing, but as the night moved on other people began to migrate into the team party. Just as things were starting to get hopping, Robin Yount showed up, in the company of catcher Rick Dempsey. But Robin—as a joke—was dressed in drag. From a distance a slightly impaired relief pitcher stared at the newcomer in the black dress and slurred, "Oh, man…She looks good. I want to get some of that."

The pitcher had to be informed that the object of his affection was actually his center fielder. Again, it was another successful team party.

Players today are much more health-conscious than they were in my generation. Nutrition is more of an emphasis now. You don't go out for steaks and scotch every night. You see guys eating more healthy food whether in the clubhouse or on their own. In the '50s and '60s, guys were driving beer trucks during the winter. Back in those days, spring training was needed for guys to lose the weight they gained over the winter. In my era we generally tried to keep in good shape year-round. But we weren't into nutrition and weightlifting like players are now. Even weightlifting has changed. Instead of loading plates on a barbell and going to town, players today focus more on functional movements—often using body weight as resistance.

One of the biggest changes over the past 25 or 30 years has been the reduction in the number of players and coaches who smoke cigarettes. I remember my first time in big league camp. I was playing catch next to Ted Simmons, and he had a cigarette in the web of his catcher's mitt and he was smoking between throws. Guys would stand in the outfield during batting practice and they would be smoking as discreetly as possible. Though players still use chewing tobacco, clubs don't provide it any more. Teams used to provide chew and cigarettes. "It's amazing how much the game has changed," former Brewers trainer John Adam recalled. "My first year in 1981, head athletic trainer Freddie Frederico would give me two packs of cigarettes and a couple books of matches. There was a little ridge in the back of the bench in the dugout at County Stadium. It was just big enough to put a cup of Gatorade on. I was in charge of making sure there were cigarettes and matches. Between innings, guys would grab them and head up the tunnel and smoke."

I know that Gorman Thomas, Ted Simmons, Charlie Moore, Rick Manning, and others were known for a smoke break. In the interest of true disclosure, I must confess that I had a heater or two myself during the course of a game. It didn't stop there, though. "We used to have guys smoking on the plane," Adam said. "You'd get off the flight, and your clothes would just stink."

Adam recalled a hilarious story that summed up the attitude of many players about smoking in the 1980s. "We were at spring training in Sun City, I think it was 1981," he recalled. "We had the stadium field and the back field, which we called 'Iwo Jima.' We used to take a small bus for a five-minute ride down a dirt road back there so that pitchers could do their running. At that time pitchers had to run from foul pole to foul pole. One morning early in camp, we went over there, and the guys had to do a little extra running. Everybody was dragging except Moose Haas, who always reported to camp in shape. Anyway, we got back on the bus, and everybody was in their running shoes and carrying their spikes, and I see this old pitcher we had, Reggie Cleveland, and he's got his hand stuck way up inside his cleat. I watched him, and he pulled out a crumpled cigarette. I watched him as he tried to straighten it out. He looked like a hobo. Finally, he fired it up and took a big drag. And he just held it in and exhaled. I remember Moose Haas looked at him and said, 'Oh, my gosh. If I was to do that right now, I'd barf.' Well, Reggie didn't bat an eye. He looked right at Moose and said, 'Moose, if I don't do this, I'll barf.'

The Chandler Explosion

February 26, 1986, was a quiet Thursday morning at Compadre Stadium in Chandler, Arizona. It was spring training, and we were getting ready for a pitchers' and catchers' workout at the complex, which was in its first year as home of the Brewers, who previously trained in Sun City. At that time Chandler, which is a suburb 15 miles southeast of Phoenix, was nothing but cattle farms and cotton fields. You cruised down Alma School Road, a beat-up two-lane road and arrived at Compadre Stadium. At the time the complex seemed pretty sweet. It was new. It was nothing like the spring training complexes they have today.

Compadre Stadium was in the middle of nowhere. Today, Chandler is a bustling metropolis. Back then, however, there wasn't anything special about it. Other than a golf course that was being developed across the street, there wasn't much around the ballpark. Today, Chandler is a bustling suburb. Back then, it wasn't. The clubhouse was pretty simple. There was a concrete floor and regular wooden lockers, not the cherry wood, country club models players have today. There was a hallway that housed the training room and a coaches' room, which was connected to the manager's office. It was a basic setup, but nobody complained because—compared to what we had in Sun City—Compadre Stadium seemed like the Taj Mahal. It was state-of-the-art at the time.

I arrived on February 26 a little after 8:45 AM and headed to my locker. I took off my shirt, socks, and shoes and headed into the training room to weigh myself. Daily weigh-ins were part of the routine back then. I joked around with the head athletic trainers, John Adam, and his assistant, Al Price, and headed back down the hallway to my locker.

All of a sudden…BOOM!

It was followed by a WHOOSH, and I saw a bright orange flash pass the left side of my body. I heard another boom, and then there was yelling as smoke began to fill the clubhouse. Everybody ran out and somebody—I forget who—patted my hair because they said it was smoking. The left side of my face was burned, along with my chest and stomach. The burns were just superficial. We got outside, wondering what the hell had happened. Apparently, a plumber had been working on a space heater in the coaches' room. The heater sent natural gas into the facility, and apparently a pilot light sparked the explosion. "It blew everyone off their chairs," clubhouse manager Tony Migliaccio recalled. In a radio interview that week, Ray Burris, a pitcher on that team, called it a "6.5 on the Richter scale."

Dale Sveum, who was in camp early, told the *Milwaukee Journal Sentinel*'s Tom Haudricourt that he saw the fireball rushing toward him. "I was sitting next to 'Simba' [Ted Simmons]," Sveum recalled. "I remember looking down that hallway and seeing the ball of flame coming at us. I ran out that door as fast as I could. [Rookie pitcher Bill] Wegman had nylon stirrup socks on, and they melted right on to his legs. I remember smelling guys' hair burning. We all just scattered."

Ten people were injured, including the plumber, Jeff Sutton, and third-base coach Tony Muser, who suffered second and third-degree burns over more than half his body. Manager George Bamberger and general manager Harry Dalton were slightly injured, trying to put out the flames on Sutton's clothing. "This bolt of fire came right through the door just like it went right through me and knocked me out of my chair," Bamberger told reporters that day. "Everybody was knocked to the floor…[Bullpen coach] Larry Haney was on the floor next to me [with] both arms on fire. The workman was in the doorway going out of my office, and he's completely on fire with his hair and his back and everything. Harry Dalton, the general manager, was trying to beat that out."

Tom Skibosh, the public relations director, opened the door to find Muser on fire with Bamberger and Haney trying to help. Adam was on the phone in the hallway just before the explosion. "I was going to hang up the phone on the wall," Adam said. "If I'd been in the hallway, I'd have been hit by the fireball. I heard a boom, then some yelling. And then just a little later, I heard another boom. Apparently, that was the roof. I remember when we were kids, we would light a firecracker and put a can over it. That's kind of what happened. The roof was plywood, and the explosion lifted the roof off and dropped it back down."

As you can imagine, the scene was hectic. "The electricity went out," Adam recalled. "There was a door that led to the concourse of the ballpark, but it was locked. Everybody had to leave through the main entrance. I remember getting outside and taking two steps and thinking, *I think we still have people in there.* So I went back in and it was dark, but there was an emergency light on. Through the smoke and the rubble, I saw a figure limping toward me. Then I realized it was Muser. The sprinklers are going off. It's funny what you remember, but we had just gotten—either earlier that morning or at the end of the day before—a huge delivery from the sanitary company we used for clean towels. They were still in the bundles. Tony [Migliaccio] would stack them up in wooden columns so players could grab 'em. I told Muser to get down. We came face to face, and I saw the blast had hit him from behind and I looked at his face and I could see he'd been burned. He was telling me, 'My lips are gone. My lips are gone.' The flame hit him from behind, scorched his back, and wrapped around him from the front. He kept telling me, 'I don't have any lips.'

"Now, I knew his nerve endings were exposed, and he was in pain and probably in shock. We grabbed some towels and wetted them down and laid him on his stomach because his skin was off. I just tried to settle him down while we waited for the EMTs to show up. At some point because the sprinklers had been going so long, it was starting to flood. The water in the hallway was about two inches deep. Now everybody knows when you've got burns that the worst thing that can happen is infection. I didn't want the water on the ground to get to his back, so we used towels to dam off the area around him. We made a fortress so the water wouldn't build up. I went to place his head on some towels so he could be a little more comfortable and I put my hand on his head, and his hair just crumbled under my hand. I didn't say anything, but I remember thinking, *Wow. All of his hair is fried.* It was surreal."

Helicopters took Muser and Sutton to the hospital. Muser got the worst of it. He ended up spending most of the spring at the Arizona Burn Unit and then a burn center at UC-Irvine. He had skin grafts and physical therapy and hydrotherapy and ended up missing the season.

While we stood in the parking lot, more players started to show up for the workout that wasn't going to happen that day. We had been in the new ballpark for five days, and it had almost blown up. We took a few days off for the clubhouse to be repaired. I ended up going in an ambulance and going to the hospital with minor burns on my chest and face. I was told that I had to stay off the playing field about a week because they didn't want me to get any dirt in there.

I remember just after the accident, I went to my room at the team hotel in Mesa, the Dobson Ranch Inn. (In those days, players who didn't live in Phoenix stayed at the team hotel.) I was sitting in my room with my door open. I'd called my father and my wife to tell them I was okay. My father had heard about the explosion, and someone had told him that I was seriously injured, and he was freaking out. After I called them, I was just sitting there, collecting my thoughts and trying to process what had happened, when who walked down the hall? Baseball great Reggie Jackson. He was staying at the hotel and saw me, walked in, and said, "Hey, tell me what happened." So I chatted with Reggie for a bit. It was one of those crazy things. It was just such a scary thing. I'll never forget that orange flash going by my head. I look back now and think it's just miraculous that nobody was killed.

STADIUM RANKINGS

Throughout my playing and broadcasting career, I have worked—as a player or broadcaster—in 53 different big league ballparks. People always ask me what my favorites are, so I thought I'd share my rankings here. Everybody has different things that they like about stadiums, and my criteria could be different. I like stadiums that are outside or have retractable roofs. I take into account the atmosphere of the ballpark, the location, the energy. I look at in-game entertainment, scoreboard stuff, the energy from the music. I like stadiums that have a sense of history and a good view from the booth.

There are a lot of things that go into my rankings, but I'll say this at the outset: Miller Park is my favorite ballpark to work in and it isn't even close. That's home for us. We have our crew there. We have Renee Hafemann, our stage manager, and Mike Falkner, our statistician, in the booth with us. It just has the familiarity of home. I love that we don't have to worry about rainouts or rain delays. I love the sightlines. I love the people who work there. It's my favorite. Here are the 10 best stadiums in my humble opinion.

1. Miller Park

I may be biased here, but it's home. Enough said.

2. Yankee Stadium

The original Yankee Stadium is No. 1 on my hit parade. It's because of the rich tradition and the great memories I have as a kid watching games there. I loved the façade and the stands and I loved hearing Bob Sheppard, the legendary public address announcer. I remember the first time I ever played in Yankee Stadium, I heard Sheppard say my name and I thought I had died and gone to heaven. Batting eighth. The catcher. No. 21. Bill Schroeder. No. 21. Unfortunately, I struck out four times against Phil Niekro that day. But I also had my best game at Yankee Stadium. It was Bat Day at the ballpark in 1987, and I went 4-for-4 with a base hit against one of my idols, Ron Guidry, and had a game-winning home run off Dave Righetti. I actually got to meet Sheppard and talk to him for 10 or 15 minutes. It was something I'll never forget. Had I not grown up going to games at Yankee Stadium, I might feel differently, but I loved the aura. Knowing that Ruth and DiMaggio and others played there really added to my feelings for the stadium.

3. Fenway Park

I remember watching games on TV as a kid. I saw Bucky Dent hit the home run. I saw Carl Yastrzemski swing the bat. The first time I walked out of the dugout at Fenway, I felt like I could reach out and touch the Green Monster. I'm not sure if my feet touched the ground. The history of it was big for me. In my first game, I was catching, and Yaz was at the plate. *Wow! I'm in a game with Carl Yaz.* Yaz took a 2–2 pitch right down the middle. I caught it and held it there. And the umpire, I think it was Bill Kunkel, called it a ball. I asked, "Where was that?" Yaz kind of looked at me like, Who are you, kid? He ended up drawing a walk, and I asked the ump again, "Where was that 2–2 pitch?" He told me, "Young man, if Mr. Yastrzemski doesn't swing at it with two strikes, I'm not calling it." I remember hitting a home run off Oil Can Boyd in '87 to give us a win. There were some great memories at Fenway Park.

4. Tiger Stadium

The booth at Tiger Stadium was so close to the action that you felt like you were in the batter's box. I once was hit by a foul ball off the bat of Curtis Pride. It got me on the shoulder. You just didn't have time to react.

5. Dodger Stadium

The weather is almost always perfect when you visit Dodger Stadium. I love getting there early when it's quiet. And I love the way you enter at street level and walk down. The park is older, but it's very well-kept and—as a bonus—you get to talk to legendary Vin Scully, who always remembers your name. He's an amazing man.

6. AT&T Park

Without a doubt, the view from the broadcast booth is the best in baseball. You look out at McCovey Cove, and it's just spectacular.

Here are the 53 stadiums in which I either played or broadcasted:

Miller Park (broadcast)

County Stadium (played and broadcast)

Dodger Stadium (played and broadcast)

AT&T Park (broadcast)

Candlestick Park (broadcast)

Fenway Park (played and broadcast)

Kauffman Stadium (played and broadcast)

Safeco Field (broadcast)

Kingdome (played and broadcast)

Coors Field (broacast)

Mile High Stadium (played)

PNC Park (broadcast)

Three Rivers Stadium (broadcast)

Comerica Park (broadcast)

Tiger Stadium (played and broadcast)

Wrigley Field (broadcast)

Petco Park (broadcast)

Jack Murphy/Qualcomm Stadium (broadcast)

Minute Maid Park (broadcast)

Astrodome (broadcast)

Target Field (broadcast)

Metrodome (played and broadcast)

Camden Yards (broadcast)

Memorial Stadium (played and broadcast)

Citi Field (broadcast)

Shea Stadium (broadcast)

Citzens Bank Park (broadcast)

Veterans Stadium (broadcast)

Yankee Stadium 1 (played and broadcast)

Yankee Stadium II (broadcast)

Angel Stadium (played and broadcast)

Nationals Park (broadcast)

RFK Stadium (broadcast)

Olympic Stadium (broadcast)

Globe Life Park/Ballpark at Arlington (broadcast)

Arlington Stadium (played)

Great American Ball Park (broadcast)

Riverfront/Cinergy Field (broadcast)

Chase Field (broadcast)

Progressive Field (broadcast)

Municipal Stadium (played)

Marlins Park (broadcast)

Joe Robbie/Pro Player/Dolphins Stadium (broadcast)

SkyDome/Rogers Centre (played and broadcast)

Exhibition Stadium (played)

Tropicana Field (broadcast)

U.S. Cellular Field (broadcast)

Comiskey Park (played)

Turner Field (broadcast)

Atlanta Fulton-County Stadium (broadcast)

Busch Stadium I (broadcast)

Busch Stadim II (broadcast)

Oakland Coliseum (played and broadcast)

The Sausage Race

Every ballpark in the big leagues has its unique traditions, but only Miller Park has the sausage race. In the sixth inning of every game, five young (and really fast) Brewers employees (or friends of employees) dress in sausage costumes and race around the warning track. There is Brett, the Bratwurst, who wears Lederhosen. There is Stosh, the Polish sausage, who sports dark sunglasses and a blue and red rugby shirt. There is Guido, the Italian sausage, who wears chef's garb. There is Frankie Furter, the hot dog, who wears a baseball uniform. And there is Cinco, the Chorizo, who sports a sombrero. It's an awesome tradition. Visiting players gather on the top step of the dugout to cheer, heckle, throw cups of water, and handfuls of sunflower seeds and—in one infamous case—use a bat in an effort to disrupt the race. The Racing Sausages make appearances at parades, fun runs, and other events in the Milwaukee area year-round. In 2013 a couple of costumes, which cost roughly $3,000 apiece, disappeared from a bar in Cedarburg and were returned.

Brewers players get asked about the race in nightly interviews and casual conversations with family members who want to participate. Some of them think it's hokey. New call-ups are often stunned to see the sausages whiz by their path in the on-deck circle or dugout. But they all realize that the fans love it and that the sausages are good for business. "My whole family has done it," Prince Fielder said during his tenure with the Brewers. "My kids were in the mini-race [a Sunday staple where adult sausages run a relay with younger kids in similar costumes]. My wife did it. My wife's cousin came and actually tore her ACL doing it."

Although it still elicits chuckles and cries of corny from critics, the sausage race has been imitated throughout baseball. The Nationals have a nightly Presidents Race, which features George Washington, Thomas Jefferson, William Howard Taft, and Teddy Roosevelt, who didn't win his first race until 2012. In 1999 Pittsburgh began utilizing racing pierogi, an event with six competitors: Potato Pete (blue hat), Jalapeno

Taking place during the sixth inning of every home game, the Sausage Race is a popular and renowned Brewers tradition.

Hanna (green hat), Cheese Chester (yellow hat), Sauerkraut Saul (red hat), Oliver Onion (purple hat), and Bacon Burt (orange hat). Arizona has a Legends Race featuring giant likenesses of Randy Johnson, Mark Grace, Luis Gonzalez, and Matt Williams. The Tampa Bay Rays have racing bottles of Pepsi products. The Cleveland Indians have racing hot dogs, and the Kansas City Royals have racing Heinz condiments. In Atlanta the race featured Home Depot tools. The Miami Marlins recently unveiled the Great Sea Race, featuring Bob the Shark, Julio the Octopus, Angel the Stone Crab, and Spike the Sea Dragon.

In Milwaukee the race is sponsored by my good friends at Klement's. When John, George, and Ron Klement joined forces to purchase Badger Sausage on Milwaukee's South Side in the mid-1950s, they couldn't have envisioned what the sausage race would become. The Brewers sell sausage T-shirts and toys in the clubhouse store. There is a popular 5K "Sausage Run" around the ballpark every year. "It's unique to Wisconsin, that's for sure," said Brewers manager Craig Counsell, who grew up in Milwaukee and whose father, John, worked in the Brewers' marketing department in the 1980s.

The Sausage Race has its roots with one of those dot races on the old black and white scoreboard at County Stadium. When Klement's came on board as a sponsor, the dots became sausages who ran past Milwaukee landmarks on the way to the stadium, but it was still essentially a dot race. In 1992 a Milwaukee graphic designer named Michael Dillon, who worked at McDill Design, presented an idea for a live-action race to Brewers vice president of stadium operations Gabe Paul, whose son, Jeff, worked at McDill.

The first race was on June 27, 1993. (It was supposed to occur a day earlier, but the scoreboard malfunctioned.) Dillon, who ran the first race as the bratwurst, won the three-sausage race, beating the Italian and Polish, and fans seemed to enjoy the joke. For a time the sausage race was just for Sunday games and special events. "We didn't want to wear out the welcome," said Laurel Prieb, a Brewers vice president in the 1990s.

As the race gained popularity, though, it became a fixture. At one point, the Brewers let key sponsors and friends of the club take part, but that has been limited now due to liability. A couple of players took part in the race, including Twins utility man Pat Meares, Brewers outfielder Geoff Jenkins, and pitcher Hideo Nomo, who was a huge fan of the racing sausages and ran with the blessing of then-manager Phil Garner. Media members such as Paul Sullivan (*Chicago Tribune*), T.J. Quinn and Tim Kurkjian (ESPN), and Padres TV analyst Mark Grant are among those who also have taken part in the race. I ran in it in the early 2000s as the bratwurst and finished in third place.

By the time the club moved into Miller Park, it was an everyday event. Eventually, the sausage race became a staple at spring training games at Maryvale Baseball Park, too. In 2007 the Chorizo joined the field on a permanent basis. It was added for Cerverceros Night, which celebrates the Hispanic community, but Major League Baseball needed a year to approve the new mascot.

For many parents with toddlers, the sausage race signals a time to head for the parking lot. For others it is a time to place bets on the outcome. The sausages received national attention on a warm summer day in 2003, when Pittsburgh Pirates first baseman Randall Simon conked the Italian Sausage (a college student named Mandy Block) on the head with his bat. Block tumbled to the track, scraping her knee, and knocking down Veronic Piech, who was racing as the hot dog. Simon ended up being arrested on a misdemeanor battery charge and subsequently was fined $2,000 and suspended three games by MLB for a prank that went awry. "I just looked over and saw our wieners in a wad," then-Brewers manager Ned Yost said after the game. Simon ended up paying a $432 fine for disorderly conduct and issuing an apology. As a good gesture, the next three times the Pirates were in town, Simon bought everyone hot dogs in the sections behind the visiting dugout. As an interesting side note to the Simon controversy, on the very night it took place, a Hollywood film crew was at the ballpark shooting a scene for the Bernie Mac movie *Mr. 3,000*.

Nicknames

Some of the nicknames come with a dose of great creativity or at least a compelling backstory. Some are just condensed versions of players' names. Jerry Augustine, who provides commentary on Fox Sports Wisconsin, is "Augie." Jeromy Burnitz was "Burnie." Geoff Jenkins was "Jenks." Paul Molitor was simply "Paulie" to teammates, though he was known as "the Ignitor" to fans. "Aside from it's not even being spelled right," Molitor told *Sports Illustrated* in 1993, "it's a terrible nickname. I never once entered a room and my friends said, 'Hey, it's the Ignitor!'"

Before we dive further into nicknames good and bad, know that my given name is Alfred William Schroeder III. My father is Alfred William Schroeder Jr., but for some reason everybody called him "Pete." I remember in school that they would call the roll, and if we had a different teacher that day, they'd call me "Alfred," and all the other kids would laugh. I wanted to avoid that with my son, Billy, so we named him A. William Schroeder IV. I think it's going to stop with him. I don't think he likes it too much. For much of my adult life, my nickname has been "Rock." Truth be told "Rock" is shortened from the original (and less flattering) "Rockhead."

How did I get that nickname? Although I've certainly engaged in my share of rock-headed behavior over the years, the nickname was born from a game in 1982 during my first year playing at Triple A Vancouver. The Canadians were members of the Pacific Coast League, and we played our home games at Fraser Stadium, which was located right by the Fraser River.

It was really damp there. It was always really misty, and by the seventh or eighth inning, there was a lot of dew on the grass. I was catching one night, and back then, we didn't wear helmets to catch. We used the cloth hat. And when you needed to catch a pop-up or get ready for a play at the plate, you just threw the mask aside, and all you had on your head was a cloth hat.

I'm pretty sure Frank DiPino was on the mound, and there was a base hit and a play at the plate. Kevin Bass was in the outfield and he threw the ball in, and it skipped off the wet grass, bounced up, and smacked me right in the eye. (You can still see the scar.) I had to go to the hospital. They've got socialized medicine over there, and I remember they were getting ready to shoot me with a syringe full of something—I thought it was Novocaine—and the doctor came running in and said, "No, not that!" I think somebody almost gave me a shot I wasn't supposed to get.

Anyway, I got stitched up and I went to the ballpark the next day, and Chuck Porter, a pitcher who had been in the dugout, told me, "The sound of that ball hitting your head was like a rock hitting a brick wall." From that moment my teammates started calling me "Rockhead." Some of my minor league teammates still call me that to this day, but over the years it luckily got shortened to just "Rock."

Here is a list of some memorable Brewers nicknames. Some of them are famous. Some of them are pretty obscure.

Bambi—George Bamberger

One of the more famous nicknames in Brewers history belonged to this former Baltimore Orioles pitching coach, who moved into the Milwaukee dugout in 1978, and the club became known as "Bambi's Bombers."

Boomer—George Scott

The burly first baseman—one of the more popular players in the team's infancy—got his nickname from Boston Red Sox teammate Joe Foy, and it was later popularized by Bud Collins, a columnist for *The Boston Globe*. Scott, a slugger with outstanding defensive skills, referred to his home runs as "taters" and his glove as "Black Beauty."

The Kid—Robin Yount

What else would you call a guy who made his big league debut at age 18? After he finished playing, he was "the Kid in the Hall" because everything in his career pointed to Cooperstown. His teammates called him Tito.

Tony Plush—Nyjer Morgan

It's rare in baseball for a player to conjure up his own nickname, but Morgan was certainly a unique soul. The man who delivered the game-winning hit in Game 5 of the 2011 National League Divisional Series against Arizona was "Tony Clutch," but he referred to "Tony Plush" as his "gentleman's name," something he and his buddies conjured when they hit the clubs and bars in the offseason.

The eccentric Nyjer Morgan is a man of many personalities and nicknames.
(Courtesy: David Bernacchi)

This led to many derivations:

Tony Hush—He used this when he wasn't talking to the media.

Tony Gumbo—Some thought he meant "Gumbel" in reference to the smooth-talking broadcast brothers Bryant and Greg, but Morgan used this name when he was being a "true professional" or a "man about town."

Tony Tombstone—When the Brewers dressed in Western attire for a road trip, Morgan became Tony Tombstone. "Don't be fooled by his name or his wardrobe, Tony Tombstone is the city slicker, the street-smart suit with a heart of gold, who when you least expect it, will rope you in with his charm and wit."

Mr. Eezzy Breezy—The origin was unknown, but you know he's chill.

Antonio Picante—This was a Latin cousin of Tony Plush.

Morgan and his alter-egos weren't in Milwaukee long, but they are remembered fondly.

Simba—Ted Simmons

The switch-hitting catcher once had a mane of shoulder-length hair, which earned him the lion nickname. He was king of the jungle on the field and in the clubhouse and was a big influence on me.

Gumby/Dog/Klinger—Jim Gantner

You have to be a popular player with a long career to have more than one nickname. Gantner, who hails from tiny Eden, Wisconsin, was both. When teammates noticed that his eyelids resembled the cartoon character Gumby, that nickname was a natural. It seemed to fit, too, because Gantner was famous for humorous quotes: "You've got to play the games on the palms of your feet," and "that's construction," when he meant obstruction. The nickname "Dog," which is still used by Robin Yount to this day, was a reference to Gantner's determination. "Klinger," a tribute to Jamie Farr's cross-dressing corporal character in *M*A*S*H*, was bestowed by Hall of Famer Rollie Fingers.

Rooster—Rob Deer

Best known for his Easter Sunday homer in 1987—and the *Sports Illustrated* cover—Deer was called this because of his shock of red hair.

Grumpy Rooster—Craig Counsell

The current Brewers manager was dubbed "Grumpy Rooster" because he had a tendency to show up for spring training with his hair uncombed and was often a bit terse until he got a cup of coffee in his system.

Grumpy—Mark Reynolds

Reynolds was actually a pretty agreeable fellow, but he was quiet and a bit downcast, and some took to calling him "Grumpy."

Scrap Iron—Phil Garner

Because of his scrappy, gritty style of play, Garner earned the nickname "Scrap Iron," which was fitting when he helped the Pittsburgh Pirates win the 1979 World Series.

Mad Dog—Mike Maddux

The Brewers pitching coach and brother of Hall of Famer Greg Maddux had a nickname that played on his last name.

El Caballo—Carlos Lee

"The Horse" was a fitting nickname for this slugging left fielder, who raised horses and cattle at nine ranches in his native Panama and also at Slugger Ranch in Texas. During his time in Milwaukee, part of the stands in left field was dubbed "Caballo's Corner."

Muggsy—Gary Allenson

The former Brewers third-base coach, who spent much of his big league career with the Boston Red Sox, got the nickname as a minor leaguer because he was always getting his face and uniform dirty with headfirst slides. As is often the case, the moniker extended to his family. His father became "Big Muggs," his mom was "Mrs. Muggs," and his brother became "Middle Muggs."

Hondo—Frank Howard

By the time he was a Brewers coach, everyone called him "Hondo," which was given to him because of his resemblance to the title character in a 1953 John Wayne movie. When he was hitting homers for the

Washington Senators, though, he was called "the Capital Punisher" and "the Washington Monument." He was 6'7" and 255 pounds, so he was the biggest player of his time—and probably still would be today. Hondo was such an interesting guy. He was our hitting coach, and I'd be struggling and ask what I could do and he'd say, "Son, there is nothing that a week to 10 days of 2-for-4s can't fix." We would have early batting practice on the road, and I would go out to warm up and put down a bunt or two, and he'd say, "Son, don't worry about the bunts. You're not going to bunt. Just hook about 50 balls around that foul pole."

I can't imagine anyone saying that nowadays. It's still funny. Hondo had a million sayings. He would grab a fungo and say, "Tie that kid down at shortstop. I'm going to hit him some 'blister balls.'" I remember he would tell Paul Molitor, "Go get on base, so my fat asses can knock you in." Hondo loved his cigars, too. When we were in Baltimore one time, the fire alarm went off at three in the morning. Apparently, Hondo had walked into the elevator with a big stogie. I remember we were all outside while the fire trucks came. It was crazy.

Captain Sal—Sal Bando

This was an obvious choice. Bando, who signed with the Brewers in the late 1970s and was general manager in the 1990s, was captain of the A's powerhouse teams in the early 1970s.

Tiny—Mike Felder

This was a pretty obvious nickname for a guy who was 5'8" and weighed about 150 pounds.

Stormin' Gorman/ Spike—Gorman Thomas

Fans came to see him play to do three things: hit home runs, strike out, and crash into outfield walls while making catches. "Stormin' Gorman," though, was a bit of a mouthful for the clubhouse, so many of his former teammates refer to him by the name "Spike." Thomas said the name came from coach Frank Howard. "When a guy who is 6'8" and 300 pounds gives you a nickname, you don't ask why," Thomas joked.

Big Rig—Ron Villone

This reliever from the late 1990s picked up the nickname during his time in San Diego. During a road trip in Montreal, Villone and teammates were at a dance club, and the lefty ended up on the dance floor with a rather large woman. Someone shouted, "Villone is dancing with the Big Rig," and a nickname was born. It fit, too, because Villone was a burly, 6'3", 245-pounder, who played football at the University of Massachusetts-Amherst.

Stormy—David Weathers

This nickname was just a natural, and Weathers, a fun-loving reliever in the mid-to-late 1990s, embraced it. If you happen to see him watching his beloved Alabama Crimson Tide, be sure and yell at him, and he'll tell you some fun stories about playing in Milwaukee.

Skid—Don Rowe

Like for Weathers, this nickname was a natural. The pitching coach under Phil Garner, Rowe was a bit of a mad scientist with theories and warm-up exercises, but his pitchers generally enjoyed him.

Hot Nuts—Al Reyes

Nobody is sure just how Reyes got this nickname, but Bob Uecker is definitely involved in bestowing it.

Jenks/Clipper—Geoff Jenkins

Early in his Brewers career, Jenkins was known as a Brett Favre lookalike. Though the nickname "Jenks" was short and easy, some teammates called him "Clipper" because he wore No. 5, and that evoked a memory of Joe DiMaggio, the "Yankee Clipper."

Archie—Rick Manning

The affable center fielder, who is best known to Milwaukee fans as the guy who ruined Paul Molitor's 39-game hitting streak by getting a game-winning hit, was named after the New Orleans Saints quarterback. That quarterback was great in his day, but now he's more famous for being the father of Peyton and Eli Manning.

The Count—Matt Garza

With black hair and a trademark soul patch, the Brewers' right-hander bears a striking resemblance to "the Count," the vampire on *Sesame Street*. "I've also been called the 'Duke Blue Devil,'" Garza said.

The Rat—Jamie Easterly

While playing in the Carolina League in 1971, Easterly was dubbed "Rat" by teammate Stan Babieracki, who said Easterly looked like a rat and ate a lot of cheese. It's no small wonder then that Easterly ended up pitching in Wisconsin.

Meat—Allen Levrault

Levrault, a hulking right-hander from New England, was dubbed "Meat" during rookie ball as an homage to Tim Robbins' character Ebby Calvin "Nuke" LaLoosh in the movie *Bull Durham*. (Kevin Costner's character, Crash Davis, derisively called LaLoosh that.) Levrault embraced the nickname, even having it emblazoned on his glove and other equipment. During the 2000 season, he was called up to the Brewers from Triple A Indianapolis and met the big league club at the Metrodome for a game against the Twins. In his excitement to get to the clubhouse, Levrault left the big equipment bag he had brought with him in the trunk of the cab. It took him 30 minutes to realize he didn't have the bag, which contained his glove, spikes, and other essential items. The clubhouse staff scrambled to call cab companies to find the car. Finally a dispatcher called and said, "We have the bag, but we don't think it belongs to Allen Levrault; it doesn't have his name on it." Asked what was inscribed on the bag, the disapatcher replied, "Meat."

Mr. Happy—B.J. Surhoff

The former Brewers catcher and outfielder was notoriously grumpy, so teammates called him "Mr. Happy." Former manager Phil Garner once said, "B.J. could win the lottery, and he'd be mad about paying the taxes."

CoCo—Francisco Cordero

The closer on the Brewers' 2008 playoff team got his name by combining the last two letters of his first name with the first two letters of his last name.

Big Sexy—Richie Sexson

This was another obvious nickname given Sexson's name and imposing 6'8"-inch frame.

Corn Fed—Cal Eldred

This moniker, a nod to Eldred's Iowa heritage, actually had an unintentional derivation. Teammates called him "Corn Fed," but many media outlets—thanks to copy editors and spellcheckers—changed it to "Corn Field."

Moo-Moo—Glenn Braggs

Glenn Braggs was referred to this way because he could entertain the ladies "until the cows come home." He was also known as "Braggsie."

The Mayor—Fernando Vina

A popular second baseman in the mid-1990s, Vina got his nickname because he liked to shake hands with security guards, groundskeepers, clubhouse personnel, media members, and just about everybody else. It wasn't uncommon to shake Vina's hand when he walked by two or three times a day—before batting practice. Teammates also referred to Vina as "Nando," a shortened version of his first name.

The Chief—Ramon Garcia

The right-handed reliever was dubbed "Chief" and sometimes "El Jefe" because he bore a resemblance to the character of the same name from *One Flew Over the Cuckoo's Nest*.

Coop/Divot Head—Cecil Cooper

Though not terribly creative, the former nickname was popular among fans, who loved yelling "Coooooop!" when Cecil was at the plate. Gorman Thomas, the king of bestowing nicknames, also called Coop "Divot Head" because "his head looked like somebody forgot to replace a divot on a golf course."

Sweetness—Dick Davis

The outfielder liked to be called "Sweetness," but Walter Payton ended up owning that name years later.

Fruity—Scott Karl

Though some said that this nickname stemmed from Karl eating a bowl of Fruity Pebbles, others, including former teammate Steve Sparks, maintain that it is a shortened version of "Fruity Pants," a nickname whose origin is unknown.

Frenchy—Jim Lefebvre

With a name like Lefebvre, this nickname was almost unavoidable. Lefebvre was the Brewers' hitting coach and interim manager in 1999.

Scooter—Scott Fletcher

Although most baseball people know that Phil Rizzuto is "Scooter," just about anybody named "Scott" will get hit with the nickname. Scooter Gennett, the Brewers' current second baseman, also got the nickname because of his love for a Muppets character with a similar name.

Munchkin—Charlie Moore

The catcher/outfielder earned this nickname for being one of the smaller hitters in the Bambi's Bombers/Harvey's Wallbangers era.

Big Foot—Pete Ladd

A deputy sheriff/parole officer in his non-pitching time, Ladd, who filled in for Rollie Fingers during the stretch run in 1982, appropriately earned this nickname because of his size 15 EEE shoes.

Cheeser—Damian Miller

Because he hailed from the La Crosse area in western Wisconsin, he was dubbed "Cheeser" by teammates. It was a shortened version of "Cheesehead," which could have applied to Gantner, Augustine, Willie Mueller, and Paul Wagner as well.

The Mechanic—Tony Fossas

Although he didn't make the Hall of Fame as a situational lefty, Fossas had the honor of being nicknamed by a Hall of Famer. Brewers radio announcer Bob Uecker called Fossas "the Mechanic" because of his blue-collar appearance.

Hank White—Henry Blanco

The catcher with the shotgun arm was called Hank White because someone thought the translated version of his name was funny.

Spread Killer—Dave Valle

The former Brewers catcher was called this because he was known for going through the buffet line multiple times.

Bud—Chuck Hartenstein

The former Brewers pitching coach preferred Budweiser beer. He loved the Beechwood product so much that if he went to a restaurant and they didn't have it, he would leave. His wife was affectionately referred to as Bud Light.

Eddie Love—Ed Sedar

The guys call him that because of his dashing and debonair manner. He was also known as Captain Eddie. He and I have enjoyed a few Captain Morgan and Cokes on occasion.

Earth Pig—Mike Caldwell

Simba gave him that because he was known to eat very loudly.

PART III:
GREAT GAMES

Brewers Win the 1982 Pennant

October 10, 1982

The image is indelible.

It's the bottom of the seventh. The Brewers are down by a run. Cecil Cooper lashes a single to left field, motioning for the ball he hit off California Angels reliever Luis Sanchez to get down as he runs toward first base. Charlie Moore and Jim Gantner score on the play and then celebrate together at home plate as County Stadium erupts. Cooper's hit gave the Brewers a 4–3 lead they did not relinquish. Milwaukee had won the American League pennant in dramatic fashion.

The path wasn't easy. The Brewers dropped the opening two games of the best-of-five American League Championship Series in Anaheim. After fighting back to win Games 3 and 4, the Brewers faced another winner-take-all game. Pete Vuckovich, who was weeks away from being named the American League Cy Young winner, started for Milwaukee against California's Bruce Kison. Both men were throwing on three days' rest, and it showed. Vuckovich gave up three runs in four innings. Kison allowed a solo homer to Ben Oglivie, who had missed the previous games with a rib injury, in the fourth that drew Milwaukee to within 3–2.

In the fateful seventh inning, the Brewers loaded the bases with two out, and Angels manager Gene Mauch made a decision that haunts Halos fans to this day. Although Cooper's batting average was 50 points lower against lefties, Mauch stayed with the right-handed Sanchez, and Cooper burned him with an opposite-field single for the ages. "For a minute I thought it would be caught because when you hit line drives they have a tendency to hang, especially with the wind blowing in like it was," Cooper said. "That's why I was motioning for it to go down. It got down. It was one of the biggest thrills of my career."

When you watch the replay of Cooper's hit, you can see the camera shake as Gantner and Moore celebrate at home plate. That's not surprising. It was shot from the high home-plate camera, and the entire state of

Wisconsin seemed to be quaking at the time. "Charlie grabbed me. He was excited. I was excited," Gantner said. "But when we went back to the dugout, I said, 'We've got six more outs to go. We haven't won this until we get six more outs. Let's get them, then go crazy.'"

With ace Rollie Fingers, the reigning Cy Young Award winner and MVP, sidelined by injury, the Brewers held the Angels at bay for the final two innings, and the game ended on Rod Carew's ground-out to shortstop Robin Yount. Closer Pete "Big Foot" Ladd had stepped up in Fingers' place to take care of one of the all-time great hitters. "I remember thinking, *Of all the guys to be up, why Carew?*" Brewers President Bud Selig recalled later. "When he grounded the ball to Robin, it was one of the greatest moments of my life."

Tony Plush Saves the Day
October 8, 2011

Nineteen years after Cecil Cooper's single in Game 5 provided a signature moment for the Brewers in County Stadium, the team conjured more magic in Game 5 of a playoff series, this time at Miller Park. Unlike the 1982 Brewers, who were playing from behind, the 2011 Brewers won the first two games of their National League Divisional Series against the Arizona Diamondbacks and then found themselves in a do-or-die matchup in Game 5.

Because it was a playoff game, I was watching from the Fox Sports Wisconsin suite when previously infallible closer John Axford coughed up a run in the ninth inning, snapping a string of 43 consecutive saves and sending the game to the 10th inning. With one out in the home half, Carlos Gomez singled to left and stole second. Nyjer Morgan, the speedy, outspoken center fielder whose alter-ego, "Tony Plush," became a local phenomenon that summer, stepped to the plate and punched a one-hop single past Diamondbacks closer J.J. Putz into center field.

Gomez, running like the wind, slid home with the winning run as the ballpark erupted in celebration of Milwaukee's first postseason series victory since '82. "We've heard all about 1982, so it's nice to start our own legacy," slugger Ryan Braun said.

Braun nicknamed Morgan "Tony Clutch" for his exploits, but Morgan—acquired for minor leaguer Cutter Dykstra in the closing days of spring training—had been anything but clutch during the series. He was 1-for-11 in the first three games and watched from the visitor's dugout as the Brewers lost Game 4 in Arizona. Though he had doubled earlier in the game, he also popped out and snapped a bat over his knee and sent another piece of lumber sailing down the first-base line on a seventh-inning strikeout.

In the postgame hysteria after the triumphant Game 5 win, Morgan donned an Army helmet, dropped an F-bomb on live TV, and basically bopped around the clubhouse like an eight-year-old after consuming a bag of candy on Halloween night. At one point he did stand still long enough to talk about what the hit meant. His grandfather, Frank, the only member of his family who had played baseball, had passed away in May and wasn't there to see it. At one point Morgan's eyes reddened, and it wasn't from the champagne shower. "Basically, it's just everything I've had to overcome," he said, "just the stuff that people go out there and perceive about me. All my haters, I just want to show them that I can play this game. Even though I've got a fun, bubbly personality and everything like that, I still come to win and I'm a winner."

Braun and CC Brew Up a Winner

September 28, 2008

I don't know who said it first, but it is true in baseball and just about every sport under the sun: in order to win big games, you need your star players to play like stars. Brewers pitcher CC Sabathia and leftfielder

The Brewers celebrate winning Game 5 of the National League Division Series against the Arizona Diamondbacks. *(Courtesy: David Bernacchi)*

Ryan Braun got the memo on the final day of the 2008 regular season. From Little League through college and the big leagues, this day may have been the most exciting of my career. It was unbelievable.

Sabathia, pitching on three days' rest for the third straight start, shut down the Chicago Cubs. Braun belted a two-run homer in the eighth to send Milwaukee to a 3–1 victory and a share of the National League wild-card berth. When Sabathia retired Derrek Lee on a game-ending double play ball, his 122nd pitch of a heroic afternoon, the tension was still palpable.

The team and the capacity crowd watched on TV on the center-field scoreboard as the Florida Marlins beat the New York Mets 4–2, eliminating the Mets from wild-card contention and sending Milwaukee to a first-round matchup with the Philadelphia Phillies. After snapping a string of 15 non-winning seasons in 2007, the Brewers pushed their chips to the center of the table at midseason in 2008, acquiring Sabathia from the Cleveland Indians.

The hulking lefty definitely held up his end of the bargain. He made 17 starts, posting an 11–2 record with a 1.65 ERA and seven complete games. But the Brewers stumbled down the stretch, lost 11 of 14 games, and replaced manager Ned Yost with coach Dale Sveum. Needing a victory in the finale to keep their postseason dream alive, the Brewers got a gritty outing from Sabathia, who allowed his only run after an error by Prince Fielder in the second. Not only did he pitch like a champion, Sabathia narrowly missed hitting a homer and made a key defensive play when he bare-handed a comebacker hit by Koyie Hill to end the eighth. "It was his game," Sveum said afterward. "It was his year. It was his two months. It was his game to give his as long as he could possibly go."

Braun helped make sure Sabathia had a chance to finish. Silent for much of the game, the Brewers' offense came to life in the seventh when Ray Durham led off with a walk, and the next three batters walked. (It was current Brewers manager Craig Counsell who drew the free pass that scored Durham to tie the game.) With two out and Mike Cameron on first in the bottom of the eighth, Braun stepped in to face Bob Howry. Braun, who had shown a flair for the dramatic since his National League Rookie of the Year campaign in 2007, smacked the first pitch into the left-field seats for his 37th homer to give Milwaukee a 3–1 lead. "I got enough for it to be a home run," Braun said. "I wasn't sure. Once I saw [Alfonso] Soriano's number, I thought I was in pretty good shape."

Braun rounded first with his fist held high. My partner, Brian Anderson, his voice squeaking, called the shot, and thousands of Wisconsites screamed themselves hoarse.

I was down in the clubhouse for a postgame show and I'll never forget the scene. The entire team was stuffed into the dining room, watching the Mets-Marlins game. I was out in the hallway, standing next to Debbie Attanasio, the wife of our owner, Mark Attanasio. I remember telling her, "You might want to move out of the way. When this ends, you might get trampled."

The crowd watched the Mets game on the center-field scoreboard. When the Mets lost, the players came charging out of that room, and the celebration was crazy—both in the clubhouse and in the stands. Sabathia, Braun, and teammates doused fans with champagne from the top of the dugout and celebrated the end of 26 years of frustration.

"We've heard a lot about the 1982 team," Braun said. "It's nice to create a legacy of our own."

Later that night, much of the team headed to a bar on Milwaukee's East Side, where the party lasted deep into the night.

It Takes 162
October 3, 1982

It was supposed to be easy. As the 1982 regular season wound to its finish, the Brewers led the American League East by three games over the Baltimore Orioles. The only thing standing between Harvey's Wallbangers and a division title was a four-game series against the Orioles at Memorial Stadium.

Baltimore, however, won the first three games by lopsided margins of 8–3, 7–1, and 11–3, setting up a nationally televised finale pitting Orioles ace (and Jockey underwear model) Jim Palmer against Brewers veteran Don Sutton, who was picked up at the trading deadline with just such an occasion in mind. As if the winner-take-all stakes weren't high enough, the game also marked the final regular season appearance of legendary Orioles manager Earl Weaver, who was looking to delay his planned retirement with one last run to October. A crowd of 51,642 showed up ready to cap one of the more remarkable finishes in sports history.

The Brewers had other ideas.

Brewers shortstop Robin Yount, the eventual American League MVP, belted a pair of solo homers off Palmer early in the game to set the tone. He also led off the eighth inning with a triple and eventually scored to give Milwaukee a 5–1 lead. Baltimore threatened against Sutton in the bottom of the inning, but Ben Oglivie made a sliding catch to steal a hit from Joe Nolan. Sutton, who was warned early in the game after a scuff was discovered on a baseball he threw, ended up allowing eight hits but gave up just two runs. Sutton almost didn't pitch that day due to an illness. Hall of Famers find ways to get the job done. The Brewers unloaded with five more runs and ended up winning 10–2. "Let's face it, it was Robin Yount's day, not ours," Orioles right-hander Dennis Martinez said.

As the Brewers celebrated in the visitor's clubhouse, Orioles fans and executives paid tribute to Weaver. Superfan Bill Hagy did his O-R-I-O-L-E-S cheer, and the crowd roared. As it turned out, Weaver returned to the dugout in the middle of the '85 season and managed through 1986 before retiring for good.

Good-bye, Detroit
October 3, 1981

In some ways the regular-season finale in 1981 was a preview of the finale in '82.

After opening the final weekend series of the season with a victory, the Brewers needed one more victory in their final two games over the visiting Detroit Tiger to win the second-half crown, a distinction necessitated by the midseason strike that shut the game down from mid-June into August.

With the vaunted New York Yankees awaiting the winner, the Brewers and Tigers sent their respective aces—Pete Vuckovich and Jack Morris—to the mound for a Saturday afternoon matchup. Both men were tied for the American League lead with 14 wins and both were masterful early.

In the sixth inning, Kirk Gibson singled for the Tigers and scored when Cecil Cooper mishandled Richie Hebner's grounder to the right side. The Brewers answered with a rally that didn't really fit the mold of "Harvey's Wallbangers." They pushed across a pair of runs with two walks, two bunt singles, and a Gorman Thomas sacrifice fly. The ninth inning belonged to Rollie Fingers, the American League Cy Young and MVP winner that year. He retired the side and struck out the final two batters—Champ Summers and Lou Whitaker—to end the game.

Bob Uecker's radio call of the final out: "Good-bye, Detroit. Hello, New York" was an instant classic.

As Whitaker trudged toward the dugout, Ted Simmons leapt into Fingers' arms at the mound, prompting Fingers to think, *I hope he's not as heavy as he looks*, and Simmons to recall that, "He danced me around like a child. The crowd of 28,330—a total no doubt dampened by the strike earlier that summer—cheered in appreciation. The No. 1 fan, Bud Selig, led the cheers.

"As soon as Fingers struck out Whitaker, I wept like a baby," Selig afterward. "I tried to stand up, but my legs were shaking so much, I fell down. When the players came out of the dugout and waved at me, I wept again." Selig didn't get much time to dry his eyes. In the clubhouse moments later, Vuckovich and Simmons carried him into the training room and dumped him in the whirlpool.

The Brewers had posted their first winning season in 1978, winning 93 games. They improved to 95 wins a year later but didn't make the playoffs. Although they won 86 games in 1980, that was good for third place. Nobody in Milwaukee seemed to be interested in "asterisks" to mark the split-season. It was just good to be playing into October.

The Kid Hits 3,000
September 9, 1992

R obin Yount never felt comfortable in the spotlight. But in this game, he couldn't avoid it. With a single off Cleveland's Jose Mesa, Yount became the 17th player in major league history to collect 3,000 hits. That hit, on the final day of a homestand, capped a long journey for Yount, who wanted to get the milestone out of the way and do it in front of the home fans. "It almost feels like you're out there alone. It's kind of a weird feeling," he said, "at least it was for me. I remember that we were in a pennant race and I felt very uncomfortable because it seemed like the focus was on me and I felt that it should have been on the team because we had a legitimate chance to win that division that year. I found myself getting caught up in it because everyone else was caught up in it. I'll be honest—for me, it was a bit of a distraction. I can remember when I got within one or two hits, I got real angry at myself because I was distracted."

Yount got a hit in each of the first two games of the series. He was 0-for-3 in the finale against the Indians before shooting the single to right off Mesa. "It wasn't about one hit," Yount said. "It was about longevity. I had to remember that I had played 19 years, and it was silly to focus on one hit. But people made such a big deal out of it that I got caught up in it."

Brewers manager Phil Garner told reporters afterward that Yount was the most unselfish star in the game. "I believe that Robin could be two hits from 3,000 on the final day of the season and I could ask him to bunt every at-bat and he would do it, accepting that it was in the best interest of the team," he said. B.J. Surhoff agreed. "Yount is the greatest example there is—the perfect player, the ultimate competitor," he told reporters after the game. "I'm not sure all of our young players realize that, but at some point they'll look back and appreciate it."

Molitor's Streak Ends
August 26, 1987

The crowd of 11,246 who filed into County Stadium for a game between Milwaukee and Cleveland ignored day-long rains in hopes of witnessing history. History is what they got. Never in baseball history had a veteran pinch-hitter belted a game-winning single in the 10th inning and been booed by the home crowd.

But it happened to Rick Manning.

Manning's single brought Mike Felder home with the only run in a 1–0 Milwaukee victory. And the fans booed because Paul Molitor was on deck. Manning's hit simultaneously ended the game and—coupled with an outstanding effort by Indians rookie right-hander John Farrell—deprived Molitor of a fifth chance to extend his hitting streak from 39 games to 40.

When the game and the streak ended, Molitor ran with teammates to congratulate Manning and ended up being mobbed himself. "I was surprised how the congratulations went from him to me in about four or five seconds," Molitor told reporters the day after the streak. "I'd thought that might happen when we were in the clubhouse. Tony Muser [Milwaukee's third-base coach] was the first there to give me a nice warm hug around the neck."

Molitor, who was patient with reporters as the pressure of the streak mounted, admitted that a small portion of him was rooting against Manning, too. "It's human nature in a lot of ways," he said. "You could tell that by the reaction of the crowd. It just seemed that the streak was more important at that point. But it's impossible not to pull for a teammate. I just can't be disappointed when the guy in front of me gets a game-winning hit."

Manning, a popular veteran, displayed good humor about the episode. At times his self-deprecating humor almost sounded like longtime broadcaster Bob Uecker. "Normally, I'd hit into a double play in that situation," Manning told reporters the following day. "I don't know what happened." He joked about trying to wave Felder back to third base. ("He completely ignored me," Manning said.) He joked about having a clubhouse attendant start his car each day, "just in case anyone tries any funny business."

Paul Molitor singles on August 25, 1987, against the Cleveland Indians to extend his hitting streak to 39 straight games, but that streak would end the very next day.

After going 0-for-4 against Indians pitcher Farrell, who went on to manage in the big leagues for the Boston Red Sox and Toronto Blue Jays, Molitor handled the situation with his usual grace and class. Farrell, who was trying to establish himself as a big league pitcher at age 25, asked for an autographed ball for his collection. Molitor sent him one with the following inscription: "Wishing you a great career. My best always.— Paul Molitor"

Molitor began his streak on July 16, when he came off the disabled list and moved to designated hitter. He hit .415 during the streak, raising his batting average from .323 to as high as .370. In 22 of the 39 games, he had a hit by his second plate appearance. Only three times did he go down to his final at-bat. He had four hitless plate appearances in the final game—a strikeout, double-play grounder, grounder to short, and an error. In the aftermath Molitor lingered on a sixth-inning ground-out to short. "He gave me a pitch to hit," Molitor said. "I pulled off it a little and didn't get it. That happens in many at-bats during the season, but because of the circumstances, I remember it. Maybe I was a little over-anxious. But for the most part, I didn't feel nervous. I stayed relaxed because as long as the streak went, I knew it was going to end sometime."

Molitor, who was a rookie when Pete Rose embarked on the National League-record 44-game hitting streak, said the grind of the streak gave him an appreciation for what Rose and Joe DiMaggio—whose 56-gamer remains the gold standard—accomplished. In typical Molitor fashion, Paulie went out the next day and started a new streak by collecting two hits.

Shadow Dancing
May 16, 2004

In 2004 Ben Sheets produced one of the best seasons of any pitcher in Brewers' history. The former Olympic gold medal winner—and first-round draft pick—posted a 2.70 ERA and struck out a franchise-record 264 batters in 237 innings. Unfortunately, his teammates didn't approach his level of excellence. Sheets suffered from a lack of run sup-port and finished the season with a 12–14 record.

Everything was perfect, though, in a 4–1 victory on a sunny Sunday afternoon against the Braves. Sheets had a blazing fastball and a knee-buckling curve that, coupled with the shadows created by the roofline at Miller Park, made him unhittable. He struck out 18 Atlanta batters, including six of the last seven he faced and all three in the ninth inning. Normally cool and composed on the mound, Sheets admitted that he got emotional in the final moments before Johnny Estrada's game-ending whiff. "I wanted to get it for the fans as much as I wanted to get it for me," he said. "I'm not a big strikeout guy, so this is all new to me. It's pretty cool though."

Prior to this historic outing, Sheets' career high for a single game was 10. The Brewers' record was 14 set by Moose Haas against the New York Yankees on April 12, 1978. Sheets gave up three hits, but the only major blemish on his mark was a solo homer by Andruw Jones, who smacked an 0–2 pitch over the wall in center in the seventh. Sheets threw 116 pitches—91 for strikes. "It's unbelievable that you strike out that many people, and your pitch count is there," Brewers pitching coach Mike Maddux said. "It's a testament to throwing the ball over the plate and making it happen."

Braves manager Bobby Cox, whose pitchers were known to be given some latitude by umpires over the years, complained to plate umpire Doug Eddings about what Cox thought was a generous strike zone. But it didn't matter. The Brewers followed a perfect formula for a sunny day at the ballpark, jumping to a 3–0 lead and coasting to victory before a crowd of 20,654.

County Stadium Finale

September 28, 2000

In the final game at Milwaukee County Stadium, the Brewers lost to the Cincinnati Reds 8–1. Nobody seemed to care. The capacity crowd of 56,354 came to bask in the history of the ballpark, which served as home to the Milwaukee Braves, Brewers, the Green Bay Packers, and numerous concerts and civic events. "It was here that boys became men," Bob Uecker said in opening a ceremony that approached two hours. "And men became champions, and champions became legends."

More than 40 former Brewers, Braves, and Packers took part in the ceremony. The guest list included Henry Aaron, Del Crandall, Warren Spahn, Robin Yount, Paul Molitor, Rollie Fingers, Jim Gantner, Willie Davis, Andy Pafko, Bart Starr, Sixto Lezcano, Lew Burdette, and Jim Taylor.

Grand Salami
September 25, 2008

Ryan Braun's ribs were hurting, and he was 0-for-4 in the game when he stepped to the plate with the bases loaded in the bottom of the 10th inning. With the score tied 1–1 and the Brewers desperately needing a victory to keep pace with the New York Mets in the National League wild-card race, Braun stepped into a 2–2 pitch from Jesse Chavez and hammered the ball deep into left field. It was the first grand slam of his career and the first of the season for the Brewers. "There's no better feeling in the world than a walk-off home run—especially based on the situation that we're in," Braun said after the game.

Braun's homer added to the drama that began when Prince Fielder belted a game-winner in the bottom of the ninth to hand the Brewers a 7–5 victory against the Pittsburgh Pirates two nights earlier. Fielder's homer, his 34th of the year, came off T.J. Beam. Like Braun, Fielder had been 0-for-4 heading into the big at-bat. Both homers were iconic. Braun held his bat high as he headed to first; Fielder untucked his shirt as he headed to second. Those magic moments created momentum heading into the final series with Chicago.

The Hit Parade
August 28, 1992

On paper the Brewers' game against the Toronto Blue Jays didn't look promising. Milwaukee had lost five in a row overall and 10 in a row on the road. Toronto starter Jimmy Key was coming off a pair of solid outings. But the planets aligned, and the Brewers bashed out 31 hits—an American League record—en route to a 22–2 victory. "I'm at a loss to explain it," Brewers skipper Phil Garner said, adding that he wasn't "comfortable" until his team reached 15 runs.

Kevin Seitzer and Scott Fletcher each had five hits in the victory, while Pat Listach and Darryl Hamilton added four each. Fletcher and Hamilton each drove in five runs, while Paul Molitor knocked in four. Two interesting footnotes to this game: Robin Yount was limited to one hit, moving him 13 away from the 3,000 mark, and, pitcher David Cone, acquired in a trade earlier in the week, watched from Toronto's dugout and made his Blue Jays debut the next day.

Toronto got the last laugh, though, holding off a late charge from the Brewers to win the American League East.

The Future Arrives

June 25, 2005

It isn't often that you feel a playoff atmosphere during late June. This game, though, was one of the more exciting midseason contests I've ever seen. The Brewers were playing the Minnesota Twins, a friendly rivalry that always created a little extra buzz in the ballpark. It was a beautiful summer night. Miller Park was packed.

Johan Santana, one of the better lefties in the league, started for Minnesota. Rookie second baseman Rickie Weeks took him deep in the first inning for his first big league homer. The capacity crowd of 44,685 went wild, but that was nothing compared to what happened later.

Prince Fielder stepped up as a pinch-hitter in the sixth inning. The Brewers were trailing 5–4 at the time. With two men on, Fielder stepped into a pitch from Jesse Crain and hammered a homer to left-center to give his team a 7–4 lead. Daron Sutton had a classic call: "Career home run No. 1 for a man who is Prince but soon will be king."

Milwaukee hung on to win the game 7–6 with emerging star Derrick Turnbow retiring the heart of the Minnesota order for his 14th save. There was excitement off the field that night, too. The Brewers introduced their No. 1 draft pick, a third baseman from the University of Miami named Ryan Braun.

Friday Night Fights
July 27, 1979

Cecil Cooper called it "one of the most exciting nights of my career." He'd get little argument from the 47,928 spectators who saw the Brewers battle to a 6–5 victory against the hated world champion New York Yankees. In the opener of a three-game series played on a sultry 86-degree night, Cooper hit three homers, including a two-out, game-winner off Goose Gossage in the bottom of the ninth inning.

That was just the final firework of the game. Cooper's first homer, a two-run shot off Ed Figueroa in the first inning, gave Milwaukee a 2–1 lead. Two innings later Figueroa greeted Cooper with a brushback pitch. Brewers lefty Mike Caldwell, dubbed the "Yankee Killer" because of his success against the Bronx Bombers, responded by dusting New York slugger Reggie Jackson twice during an at-bat that ended with a pop-up to third base.

As Sal Bando camped under the ball, Jackson flipped his bat toward the mound, where Caldwell picked it up and tried to smash it. Jackson rounded first and then headed for the mound, where he grabbed Caldwell by the neck. As the benches emptied, the two toppled over. It took 10 minutes for order to be restored. Jackson was ejected. Yankees manager Billy Martin protested and then almost jumped into the stands to take on some fans who were throwing garbage and insults his way.

The game seesawed back and forth with the Yankees tying the score 5–5 on a two-run homer by Willie Randolph in the eighth. With two out in the bottom of the ninth, Cooper homered on a 1–2 pitch from Gossage.

Three years later, Cooper belted a single that lifted the Brewers to the American League pennant. The three-homer game, though, ranked right behind that one in terms of excitement. The Brewers ended up sweeping the series with the finale also marred by a brawl that began when Lou Piniella slid into Jim Gantner at third base.

May Marathon

May 8, 1984

Outside of Juan Nieves' no-hitter, the most historically significant game that I was part of had to be the matchup with the Chicago White Sox at Comiskey Park. It was—and remains today—the longest game in major league history. The White Sox beat us 7–6 in a game that lasted 25 innings, eight hours, six minutes and stretched out into a second day.

I have to admit I don't remember a lot of details. I know that I didn't start behind the plate. Jim Sundberg did, but I entered the game in the bottom of the 13th and ended up catching the rest of the way. I know we had plenty of chances to win. We scored two runs in the top of the ninth inning with Robin Yount hitting a double, stealing third, and scoring on an error, and Ben Oglivie knocked in a run with a single. But with the bottom of their order batting, the White Sox scratched two runs off Rollie Fingers to tie the game.

The rest is pretty much a blur. I know the game was suspended when we hit the 1:00 AM curfew in the top of the 18th inning with the score 3–3. We came back the next day, picked up where we left off. Ben Oglivie hit a three-run homer in the 19th inning, but the Sox got three in the bottom when third baseman Randy Ready fielded a routine grounder and made a wild throw into the sixth row of the stands. We ended up losing when Harold Baines homered off Chuck Porter in the bottom of the 25th inning. Tom Seaver pitched the final inning for the White Sox and got the win. Then we took a little break, and he came back and started the second game and won that, too. He pitched eight and one-third innings in the second game, winning 5–4.

The second game lasted only two hours and nine minutes, so you know we just wanted to get out of there. I didn't start the next game, and neither did White Sox veteran Carlton Fisk. That's okay, though, because Fisk caught all 25 innings of the opener. And he ended up pinch running and finishing the second game, too.

Nieves' No-Hitter
April 15, 1987

It was a gray, damp, drizzly, and chilly Wednesday afternoon when I boarded the bus with my teammates at the Cross Keys Hotel in Baltimore and headed for Memorial Stadium. Little did I know I was about to become part of history.

The Brew Crew was on a roll. We'd won our first eight games of the season and were going to try to sweep the finale of a three-game series against the Orioles. Mike Flanagan, a veteran lefty, was starting for Baltimore that night. As a right-handed-hitting backup catcher, I often got the call to start against tough lefties. It wasn't a backup or straight platoon situation. Tom Trebelhorn sometimes just used B.J. Surhoff against soft-tossing left-handed pitchers. But my name wasn't on the lineup card posted in the clubhouse that afternoon. Surhoff was going to get the start.

I was a bit bummed about that because I always had family visit me in Baltimore, and my father was in town for the series. He actually thought about leaving before the last game and driving back to New Jersey. I went about my pregame routine as normal. During batting practice manager Tom Trebelhorn came up to me and said, "Billy, you're going to be catching tonight."

Apparently, B.J. had visited a dentist and undergone a root canal procedure that morning and he wasn't feeling good. At about that time, Tom Flaherty, the beat reporter from *The Milwaukee Journal*, came up to me and said, "You guys are 8–0, and we're running out of things to write about. There is nothing negative going on. Give us something to write about tonight, will you?"

I had a great relationship with Tom, whose nickname was "Flaggs." Things were different in those days. The writers flew on the plane with us. They stayed at our hotels. The player-writer dynamic wasn't as confrontational or adversarial as it seems to be in the era of the Internet, social media, and tabloid-style journalism. We trusted them. We'd have a drink with them once in awhile. There was a "drinks on the table" rule that nothing said was printable. You could be frank with them and not get burned. Anyway, I told Flaggs, "We'll try to give you something to write about," and went about my game preparation.

He got something newsworthy indeed as Juan Nieves went out and threw a no-hitter that night. The first—and to date the only—no-hitter in Brewers franchise history ended with a 7–0 score and was punctuated by Robin Yount's game-ending diving catch in center field.

After taking my pregame swings in the cage, I went out to the bull-pen to catch the last 20 pitches of Juan's warm-up. That's always important because you get a sense for what a guy has got that day. As I recall Juan's stuff wasn't anything out of the ordinary. It was actually a pretty typical Juan Nieves warm-up session. The ball was moving pretty good as it always did. He wasn't an easy guy to catch because he had good movement but didn't always know where the ball was going. He had a really heavy fastball. He threw a curveball. He mixed in a change-up once in a while and an occasional slider. A lot of times, there is no correlation between how a guy throws in the bullpen before a game and what happens on the mound. But the ball was moving a lot before the game, and I felt pretty good.

I don't know if it was the dreary, chilly weather, the off-and-on drizzle, or an after-effect of Income Tax Day, but the crowd seemed smaller than the announced total of 11,407. There wasn't a lot of juice in the ballpark. The first three innings were pretty quiet. Early on, it was clear that Juan was struggling with his secondary pitches, though he worked a three-up, three-down first inning. In the second inning, Eddie Murray led off with a sinking liner to left. Jim Paciorek made a terrific catch, which set a tone for later. A batter later Nieves walked Ray Knight but got Lee Lacy to fly out. With two out in the third inning, Juan walked Ken Gerhart but struck out Rick Burleson to end the inning. In the fourth inning, Paul Molitor made a great play to take a hit away from Cal Ripken Jr. In the fifth inning, Lee Lacy walked, but Paulie made another great play to take a hit away from Floyd Rayford. From there, Juan took over. "I had a mediocre fastball, and my slider was awful," Nieves told reporters after the game. "I just went after them in the final three innings, and my slider finally showed up."

I would respectfully disagree with that assessment. I thought the fastball was darting and sinking and had a lot of zip. He walked a few guys, but he was pretty dominant. John Shelby, who has been a coach for the Brewers in recent years, was in Baltimore's lineup that day, and he agreed. "Juan was one of the toughest left-handed pitchers I faced," Shelby said. "He had a nice, hard breaking ball, and I know he had a really good fastball. His release—for whatever reason—I thought I was on the ball and it was already by me. Unfortunately, I walked back to the dugout three times [in that game]. I can't remember if I even fouled a ball off against him that night."

Flanagan wasn't bad either. We didn't do anything against the Orioles starter until the fourth inning, when Dale Sveum hit a homer to give us a 1–0 lead. In the seventh inning, Paciorek doubled, and I reached on a bunt single, moving him to third. With one out Paul Molitor doubled to drive us both in and send Flanagan to the showers. We ended up scoring four runs off his replacement, Dave Schmidt, with the big blow coming on Greg Brock's three-run homer in the eighth.

Glenn Braggs hit a homer in the top of the ninth to make the score 7–0. We were excited for Braggsie, but we didn't need the run, and I was feeling kind of bad for Juan. The poor guy had been sitting by himself in the dugout for the last three innings. Nobody wanted to talk to him because that's the tradition in baseball. Jim Paschke, who would later be my first broadcast partner, was in the TV booth with Mike Hegan that night, and they got criticized for not mentioning the no-hitter.

Shelby said the Orioles were talking about it. "As the game was going on, everybody knew he had a good game going," Shelby said. "He wasn't one of those little soft-throwers. Before you knew it, you looked up and it was the seventh inning. Sometimes, guys say amongst themselves, 'Hey we need to get something going.' He never backed down. From the first inning to the end of the game, his stuff was just magnificent. He was poised. He was focused. It wasn't one of those nights where you say, 'We need to get some hits or we're going to get no-hit.' It sort of just happened. We were hoping somebody would get something going. The way my at-bats were going, I knew it wasn't going to be me."

The tension built in the ninth inning. Gerhart grounded out, Burleson lined out, and we fell behind Ripken in the count 2–0. I didn't want to see the no-hitter end with Ripken hammering a fastball. I wanted to be careful, and we ended up walking him. Of course, that meant facing another future Hall of Famer, Eddie Murray. Hitting from the right side, Eddie jumped on the first pitch, hit a line drive to center, and Paschke made the call: "Hit in the air...Yount...makes a *great catch*! Juan Nieves has thrown the first no-hitter in Milwaukee Brewers history!"

"That's the thing I remember most about that game," Shelby said. "It was Robin Yount running across the outfield, making that catch to end it." Once Robin made the catch, I ran to the mound. Nieves had his back to me. I think he was looking for Molitor to give him a hug. I guess I understand that. If I'm Juan Nieves, and I just threw a no-hitter and was looking for someone to go crazy with, I'd be looking for Molitor, too, rather than me. If you see the picture, Nieves and Molitor are hugging, and I'm behind them on the mound. "I didn't really think about the no-hitter until the last out, when all of my teammates started tackling me," Juan told reporters after the game in one of the least believable postgame comments in baseball history.

Asked about the catch, Robin said: "I didn't have time to think," Yount said. "I wasn't going to do anything but catch it. You don't think about it; you just react. I'm just happy we accomplished a no-hitter."

Years later, Robin admitted that he probably didn't need to dive. I don't know about that. I just know it was a great catch. "When it came off the bat, it started to hang a little bit, and I thought Robin wouldn't have any problem with it," Trebelhorn told reporters afterward. "Then it started to die and I thought, *Oh gee, there goes the kid's no-hitter.* It was just a remarkable game." But Cal Ripken Sr., the Orioles' manager, didn't think the ball would drop. "The guy's a pretty good center fielder, and when he gets a jump like that, he's going to catch it," Ripken said.

As you can imagine, the clubhouse was pretty crazy after the game. It was getaway day, which meant we were heading home to Milwaukee right after the game. We were 9–0. We'd just had a 22-year-old left-hander in his second big-league season throw the first no-hitter in franchise history and the first by a pitcher from Puerto Rico. Needless to say, we were feeling pretty good. One of our traditions on that team was to give away postgame awards. Rick Manning was usually the master of ceremonies. We had things like a Funky Hank award if you took a bad swing. If you made a dumb play, you had to carry a toilet seat around. Well, the Star of the Game award was—how can I say this politely?—it was a sex toy known as the "John Rambone Award."

The star of the game put it in his locker. After the game ESPN interviewed Nieves, and it was visible in his locker. I'm pretty sure Harry Dalton, our general manager, tried to move it out of the shot. But you could still see it. When we got back to Milwaukee, there were a lot of people waiting at the airport to greet us. Everyone was excited. I remember Flaggs came up to me and said, "Thanks for giving us something great to write about."

Before the next game at County Stadium, they had a big press conference in the Brewers dining room. It's where they did all the big interviews at that time. Somebody asked Juan about the no-hitter, and he said something like, "Yeah, it was a great day. I had good stuff and me and the catcher were really on the same page." He never mentioned my name. From that day forward, my mother did not like Juan Nieves. I am forever known as "the Catcher" in Brewers history that caught a no-hitter and went unnamed in the national media. It was a lot of fun, though. I caught a no-hitter on a day I didn't even expect to be in the lineup. You can't take that away from me.

CC's Near No-No
August 31, 2008

As much as I enjoy the distinction of being the only catcher in Brewers history to have been behind the plate for a no-hitter, I wish I had Jason Kendall to keep me company on that list.

In the middle of a historic run that will go down as one of the greatest individual performances in franchise history, CC Sabathia threw a one-hitter against the Pittsburgh Pirates at PNC Park. It should have been a no-hitter. Tom Haudricourt put it best in his game story the next day for the *Milwaukee Journal Sentinel*: "Only one man was capable of stopping CC Sabathia from throwing a no-hitter Sunday afternoon against the Pittsburgh Pirates. Introducing Bob Webb."

Webb was the official scorer who kept Sabathia from joining fellow southpaw Juan Nieves in the Brewers' history book. In the fifth inning that Sunday afternoon in Pittsburgh, Pirates third baseman Andy LaRoche hit a check-swing dribbler to the left side of the infield. Sabathia, an agile fielder despite his size, tried to pick up the ball with his bare hand but dropped it. Webb ruled the play a hit almost immediately. Brewers media relations assistant John Steinmiller asked him to reconsider, so he looked at a video replay the following inning and declined to change the call.

Needless to say, the Brewers weren't happy. Things got even more salty when Sabathia closed out a one-hitter and a 7–0 victory. (Ironically, that was the score of Nieves' no-hitter April 15, 1987, in Baltimore.) "That's a joke," seethed Brewers manager Ned Yost said after the game.

"That wasn't even close. Whoever the scorekeeper was absolutely denied Major League Baseball a nice no-hitter right there. That's sad. It's just sad. He accomplished a no-hitter and wasn't given what he deserved. We had a great game today. It's too bad the scorekeeper had to put a damper on it. I feel horrible for CC."

The Brewers appealed the play to MLB offices, but Webb's decision was upheld. Sabathia was left with a one-hit, three-walk, 11-strikeout game for his mantle. "The play came off the bat. It was a spinning ball to the right of a left-handed pitcher," Webb told a pool reporter after the game. "In my opinion it's not an ordinary play to make. It was difficult both because of the spin and because he has to make the play and turn completely around. The runner was well down the line. It would have been a really difficult play to make to get him. The standard for a hit or an error is an ordinary effort. In my view it was a hit as a result of that standard. I called it immediately, believed it was a hit. I think that's a hit in every circumstance."

Yost and the Brewers disagreed. "That's a play CC makes easily," Yost said, "not even close. If you know baseball at all, that's a play that has to be made and that's a play that can be made very simply. He rushed it. If he picks that ball up, he throws him out by 10 feet."

Sabathia, who was spectacular during the Brewers' drive to the playoffs, didn't complain.

"The ball was still rolling," he told reporters after the game. "I probably should have picked it up with my glove. If I did, we wouldn't be having this conversation."

Easter Sunday '87
April 19, 1987

When you mention the words "Easter Sunday" to Brewers fans of a certain vintage, they invariably flash back to April 19, 1987. We had won our first 11 games to open the season. Juan Nieves had thrown his no-hitter less than a week earlier. It was a beautiful, sunny, and warm day at County Stadium. Oh, and we beat the Texas Rangers 6–4, coming back from a three-run deficit in the bottom of the ninth inning on electrifying home runs from Rob Deer and Dale Sveum. "Every little ingredient was in place that day," recalled trainer John Adam. "We had the winning streak. We had an absolutely phenomenal weather day. We had a great crowd. We had up-and-coming players in Rooster [Deer] and Sveum come through with big home runs. It has to be one of the greatest games in franchise history."

Indeed. The Brewers, whose hot start was the talk of the sports world, didn't do much against Rangers starter Jose Guzman. The crowd of 29,000-plus was pretty quiet. When we retired the side in the top of the ninth, the fans—probably sensing the end of the streak—gave a big ovation. With hard-throwing lefty Mitch Williams on the mound, Glenn Braggs led off with a walk and moved to second on Greg Brock's single. After Cecil Cooper flew out to center, Deer came to the plate.

Texas manager Bobby Valentine called Greg Harris in from the bullpen. The veteran threw a first-pitch curveball, and Deer took a big hack and missed. Emboldened by the success of that pitch and knowing that "Rooster" liked to chase breaking balls, Harris threw another hook. Bob Uecker's call of the play prompted people in their cars to honk their horns and folks in the backyard to high-five each other: "A curveball drilled to deep left...way, way, way out of here and gone for Deer, and they have tied it at four! Whoaaaa, whoa!"

Deer's homer, which seemed like it was going to clear the bleachers despite a strong wind blowing in from left field, had the entire state of Wisconsin going crazy, but the party was just getting started. Harris struck out B.J. Surhoff, but Jim Gantner worked the count full and drew a walk, bringing Sveum to the plate. Sveum also worked the count to 3–2 before making history. "A swing and a fly ball, right field and deep," said Uecker before invoking the home run call that became his signature. "Get up, get up, and get out of here! Gone for Sveum, and they've done it again! Twelve in a row on a two-run blast by Sveum to win it! Oh my goodness! Holy cow, do you believe it?"

The crowd at the ballpark, which included 16-year-old Craig Counsell, went crazy. "It was one of those magical days at the ballpark," said the manager, who watched from a seat near the Brewers' dugout.

Sveum got two curtain calls from the crowd and then popped out of the dugout a third time with Deer, who was featured on the cover of *Sports Illustrated* that week under the headline "Brewing Up a Storm—Rob Deer of the Amazing Milwaukee Brewers." Deer, who visits Milwaukee regularly, is reminded about Easter Sunday almost every time. Asked how many times he's watched the replay of that ninth inning comeback, he doesn't hesitate. "Thousands," he said. "There's always something different you see, that you pick out from it. I forgot about this, but if you see Dale hitting the home run, he comes home and runs into me. When he runs into me, he hits me in the nose with his helmet, and I went back to the dugout, and my nose was bleeding like crazy. I got smoked in the face and I didn't even care. There's blood all over the place, and I'm running back like, 'Yeah!'"

The fans were jubilant in part because they were hungry. Part of the reason for the excitement heading into that game was a promise by a local restaurant chain, George Webb, to give out free hamburgers if the Brewers ever won 12 in a row. According to local legend, when the Brewers played in the American Association in the 1940s, George Webb predicted the team would win 17 straight games. When the Braves came to Milwaukee in 1953, the prediction was revised to 12 and was used in newspaper ads. True to its word, the Webb chain handed out nearly 170,000 free burgers a few days after Sveum's homer ensured victory No. 12. The fans were giddy about that. The players were equally happy. "When that game ended, I saw something that I'd never seen before in all my years in baseball," Adam said. "The guys came up the tunnel to the clubhouse and they were all screaming and hollering, and then out of nowhere, everyone just started clapping. They gave each other a round of applause. It was like they didn't know what else to do. It was just a sign of sheer joy and happiness."

There was an element of giddiness before the game, too, thanks to Adam and his Easter egg hunt. "Before we broke camp that year, I had my wife, Patty, and my daughter, Jackie, dye Easter eggs," Adam said. "I had them do one for every player. Some had numbers on them and some had nicknames. I told Tony [Migliaccio] to pack them in a road case, but I didn't know what to do with them. I was probably just going to put them in each guy's locker. When we got to Easter Sunday, I was probably being stupid, hungover, or both, and I decided we'd have an Easter egg hunt. While the guys were out for batting practice, Tony and a couple clubhouse kids and I hid the eggs. When the guys came up to the clubhouse from BP, I was waiting at the door and I said, 'We're having an Easter egg hunt. Everybody has to find their egg. The only rule is that if you see an egg that is not yours, don't say anything.' Well, guys were swearing at me and blowing me off. I didn't think it was going to happen."

The first players to find their eggs were pitchers Chuck Crim and Mike Birkbeck, who was the starting pitcher that day. The latter egg was in Birkbeck's locker because Adam and Migliaccio didn't want him to spend a lot of time looking for it. One by one, players started to find their eggs. "After a few minutes, the competitive spirit took over, and guys started to get into it," Adam said. "I remember Jim Gantner was eating them. He must have chugged about six when I told him, "Gumby, those are like two weeks old."

As game time approached, the only players who hadn't found their eggs were Robin Yount, Paul Molitor, and B.J. Surhoff—all of whom were in the lineup that day. "Those guys were really mad," Adam said. "They were sure I had set them up, but I hadn't. I asked Tony if he was screwing around, and he said he wasn't. I knew we hid them, and the game was about to start. At some point we found the missing eggs. One of them was in a hamper. Another was in somebody's street shoe. There were a few minutes left before the game, so I took the eggs and ran out to the dugout and onto the field. There were about 30,000 people there, and they had to be wondering who I was and what the hell I was doing.

"Anyway, I ran out to center field, right to where I thought Robin was going to stand and dropped his egg. Then I went to third base and set Molitor's egg on the bag. I didn't know what to do with B.J.'s, but I saw Larry McCoy, the home-plate umpire, in the corner of the dugout. Larry was a grouchy guy. I didn't think he was going to help, but I started to tell him what we were doing, and he just winked at me. He didn't say a word, but he opened up the ball bag that he had on his right hip. I put the egg in there, he closed the bag, and walked away.

"Well, we took the field, and Paulie found his egg and put it in his back pocket. The whole dugout was laughing. We all were watching when Robin picked his up, held it up, and spiked it into the ground. We were cracking up. When the game started and the first time there was a foul ball, B.J. reached back to get a new ball from Larry McCoy, who looked at me and [manager] Tom Trebelhorn, shrugged his shoulders, and put the egg in B.J.'s hand. B.J. went to throw it to the pitcher and did a double-clutch. He looked at the egg, looked at us, doubled over in the dugout, and fired it toward the bench. The whole thing was hilarious. It ended up being a great footnote to the game, but the entire day I was nervous. If we had lost the game, I figured people would blame my stupid Easter egg hunt for distracting the players and ruining everyone's concentration. Fortunately, we won. And it ended up being a great day."

All-Time Brewers Team

Left field—Geoff Jenkins

Jenks moved to right field later in his career to accommodate Ryan Braun, but he held down left field for quite a while and could be counted on for 27 homers, 85 RBIs, and some solid defense.

Center field—Gorman Thomas

We've had some tremendous defensive outfielders in Milwaukee like Marquis Grissom, Devon White, Chuckie Carr, and Carlos Gomez, but few of them had the defense, home run power, and general toughness of my pal Gorman.

Right field—Ryan Braun

He made the move from left field to right field and has been a solid, if not spectacular performer at the position. It's Braunie's bat, though, that sets him apart. No disrespect to Yount, but he might be the best Brewers hitter I've ever seen.

Third base—Paul Molitor

He was a Hall of Famer in every sense of the word. One of the smartest players I've ever seen. He was a great baserunner with quick hands. Countless times, he'd lead off a game, steal second, and score to put us up in the first inning.

Shortstop—Robin Yount

Another Hall of Famer, he had to move to the outfield midway through his career because of shoulder problems, but he won the first of his two MVPs as a shortstop, and his mix of power and defense paved the way for future generations. At one point, shortstops were light-hitting defensive specialists. After Robin and Cal Ripken Jr., teams started employing power hitters who could also pick it.

After the 2011 National League Division Series, I interview right fielder Ryan Braun, who deserves a spot on the all-time Brewers team. *(Courtesy: David Bernacchi)*

Second base—Jim Gantner

He wasn't big. He wasn't fast. But nobody was tougher than Gumby. He was a great table-setter and a great teammate.

First base—Prince Fielder

I wrestled with this one. My old teammate, Cecil Cooper, was an incredible hitter and played Gold Glove-caliber defense, but Prince had one of the best power strokes in franchise history.

Catcher—Ted Simmons

I was torn between Simba and B.J. Surhoff, who had a nice career in Milwaukee. I went with Simba, though. He was in the same class as Molitor when it came to analyzing a game. I learned a lot from being around him.

Starting pitchers

Mike Caldwell—One of the toughest competitors in team history exemplified what it meant to be a Brewers pitcher.

Ben Sheets—When he was healthy and his curveball was on, he was tough.

Zack Greinke—He had Cy Young-caliber stuff and was a threat to throw a no-hitter on any given night.

Teddy Higuera— If it wasn't for injuries, he'd have won 20 games in multiple seasons.

Yovani Gallardo—It was tough to leave CC Sabathia off this list, but Gallardo was a consistent performer and Opening Day-caliber starter during his time with the Brewers.

Closer

The Brewers have employed several notable closers, but Rollie Fingers is the standard. He won an MVP and Cy Young Award and pitched in an era when it wasn't unusual for closers to get the last six or seven outs of a game. I chose him over other favorites like Dan Plesac, Doug Jones, Francisco Cordero, John Axford, Trevor Hoffman, and Frankie Rodriguez, but at each of their peaks, I would trust any of those guys with the ball in the ninth inning.

PART IV:

BEHIND THE SCENES

Director of Clubhouse Operations

If a major league baseball team is like a family—and players and coaches and team personnel spend more time together during the course of the season than many families—the clubhouse inside the home stadium is truly a "home." Nobody has spent more time in the Brewers' home than Tony Migliaccio.

Take a look at the Brewers' director of clubhouse operations' youthful face and you'd have a hard time believing that he is approaching his 40th anniversary with the team. It all started on April 7, 1978, which was Opening Day at Milwaukee County Stadium. The Brewers beat the Baltimore Orioles 11–3 behind the pitching of Jerry Augustine, who outdueled Orioles ace Mike Flanagan with help from a nine-hit attack headlined by Sixto Lezcano's seventh-inning grand slam off Tim Stoddard.

The game marked a pair of notable debuts for the Brewers—a rookie infielder named Paul Molitor and bat boy Tony Migliaccio. "I always look back and kind of laugh," said Migliaccio (pronounced MIL-ee-AHH-chee-OH). "Molitor made the team and started at shortstop. He was a first-round draft pick, but nobody had really heard of him. He was starting at shortstop because Robin Yount had some health issues at the time. It was my first day as a batboy and a clubbie [clubhouse attendant] on the visiting side. There was a picture in the paper of Molitor making a play, and there I was the ball boy down the left-field line. I was a freshman in high school. It was Paul's first day and mine."

The following season, Migs switched to the home clubhouse, where over the next few years he worked his way up to a role as equipment manager Bob Sullivan's assistant. A budding baseball player himself, Migliaccio attended Central Arizona College and returned to Milwaukee during the summer to work for the team. "Even during the playoffs in 1982, I left school and came back and worked," he said. "The school let me go. It was kind of cool. Then I transferred back to UW-Milwaukee and finished up there. In my last semester in college, Sully passed away, and I got the head equipment job at 22 years old. For eight years I was the youngest guy doing this. Now thirty years later, I'm still here."

Migliaccio, who replaced Sullivan, is often the first guy players meet when they join the Brewers via trade, free agency, or the draft. He's dealt with hundreds of players, managers, and coaches over the years. He has been with the club in good times and bad. He's been in the clubhouse at home, on the road, and during spring training. He's made a majority of the road trips, which has put him in planes, buses, and hotels for most of his life. "I've been very lucky and fortunate to be able to do it this long," he said. "It's a great job."

Migliaccio has seen the best of times and worst of times for the Brewers. He's also seen his business—like much of the industry—undergo a remarkable expansion. "Years ago, the clubs provided players with far less than we do now," he said. "The standard was totally different. Basically, the club gave you a uniform and your hat, and that was it. Players were responsible for their own T-shirts, undergarments, socks, and whatever else the club didn't provide. In those days the clubhouse manager would buy equipment and sell it to the players as a convenience. 'Here is a jock. That's five bucks.' If players needed a T-shirt or socks, we provided them as a convenience, and the money would be taken out of a player's paycheck. It's come a long way. It's much more detailed now. The club has licensing deals with vendors that we get products from like Majestic, Rawlings, and companies like that. Back in the day, guys used to buy their own batting gloves. I would go up to Saranac Gloves in Green Bay. A hunter would bring deer skins to the factory, and they'd be tanned and made into gloves. Franklin was the first glove company to come in and start providing gloves to players and signing them to contracts. That was the start of the batting glove industry."

In the early days, teams didn't wear different jerseys for batting practice. They didn't use alternate jerseys either. Today the Brewers have home white jerseys, home blue jerseys, home throwback uniforms (1982 pinstripes), gray road jerseys, blue road jerseys, an alternate gold home top, and special occasion jerseys for things like the annual Negro League game, Cerveceros Day, camouflage for Memorial Day, a red-white-and-blue tinged July 4 jersey, and more.

When you consider that each player has at least two of every jersey, and extras are needed for midseason call-ups and acquisitions, it's a huge deal to keep track of all the jerseys, not to mention pants, jackets, and sweatshirts. "We have a lot more options now," Migliaccio said, adding that it can cost upwards of $1,500 to outfit each player. "If you look at the guys on the field now and compare it to the late 1980s, when it was all just cookie-cutter, back then most guys wore pants with a 34-inch waist and a size 44 jersey. Now we've got many options. Pants can be open-bottom or more tapered. Some guys like to wear their pants short and show some sock. Other guys don't. Twenty years ago the patterns were smaller, and things were cut tighter. Today, guys like to wear things bigger and looser. The marketing of the game has changed. We have different jackets, sweatshirts, jerseys. There is just a lot more of everything."

When fans arrive at Miller Park, they often don't know what jersey the Brewers will be wearing. Truth be told, neither do most of the players. "What most clubs do, and what we've done, is let the starting pitcher pick the jersey of the day," Migliaccio said. "I'll ask him what he wants to wear and he gets to choose, but there are some restrictions when we are on the road. The home team gets first choice. If we are on the road and the club we're playing—say it's Pittsburgh, and they are wearing a black jersey—we will have to wear our gray uniforms. You can't wear navy against black. MLB doesn't like two teams with similar colors. So I'll call their equipment guy and find out what color they are wearing. If they are wearing white, we can go with our gray or blue jersey. If we've won the last two games wearing gray, it's usually gray.

"At home we have first crack. Every Friday is retro night, so we wear pinstripes. Years ago, we didn't have so many options."

Clothing isn't the only thing that has changed in big league club-houses, which sometimes resemble restaurants. "When I started, there was food in the clubhouse, but it was very light," Migliaccio said. "We'd have cheese and crackers or things like that before the game and maybe a cooler of beer and some pretzels or chips after the game. Somewhere along the line, somebody started ordering pizzas. Now we serve full-course meals. We have top restaurants in to cater meals, even though guys might not be eating until almost 11:00 PM after a night game."

In the current baseball culture, players arrive at the clubhouse five and sometimes six hours before a game. It's not unusual for players to eat two meals—and snacks—at the ballpark. Before day games, breakfast is offered with an array of selections that would rival a hotel buffet.

I remember Gorman Thomas having two doughnuts and coffee and sucking back a cigarette while walking around in ankle weights. Despite the abundance of food available, Migliaccio said modern players are usu-ally health-conscious and try to make wise choices. "We still have some 'throwbacks' who will crush doughnuts in the morning, but some guys will just have a bagel or some cereal," he said. "It varies from person to person."

Whether you visit the clubhouse in the first week of spring train-ing or the last series of the season, when you watch Migliaccio and his staff during a workday, you'll seldom see them sit still. "When we have a night game, I'll usually crack open the doors at about 11:30 AM or noon," Migliaccio said. "We've already done the laundry and cleaning the night before, so everything is ready to go. Eric Anderson, who han-dles the food, sets that up by about 1:00 PM for coaches and players who arrive early and need something for lunch. Mainly, I'm around for play-ers if they need equipment or if they have personal stuff that they need shipped or handled. We're kind of on-call to help the players with every-thing they may need. If we have an early workout at two or three in the afternoon, we'll bring the equipment down to the dugout and get things ready for that and batting practice. After BP there is more food to be brought out, and laundry to be done. It's a constant flow of different things throughout the day. Once the game starts, we wait for the players to come in and then we clean up the mess again."

The busiest times for a clubhouse staff are arrival day and getaway day. When the Brewers get home from a trip, clubhouse staffers will often meet the plane at the airport and bring equipment back to unpack it, do laundry, and prepare for the next game. That work often takes place between 2:00 AM and 5:00 AM, depending on when the team arrives.

On getaway day before a road trip, the clubhouse crew really kicks into gear. "When the game starts on the last day of a homestand, we'll pull out each player's travel bag, put it in front of his locker, and go through and put all their uniforms for the road: two pair of road pants, two road jerseys, and the BP shirt. If it's early in the year, we'll pack their heavy coat and fleece and cold weather gear. A lot of guys tend to forget that part of it. Then you get to a city, and 10 guys don't have a warm jacket. As they come off the field after a game, the helmets get packed in a bag for the trip, the bats get zipped up and locked up. The players are responsible for packing their glove, batting gloves, toiletries, shower shoes, undergarments, and whatever else they want to take. The things they wore in the game are thrown into a "wet bag" or travel hamper. It's taken to the next city, where the visiting clubhouse crew will wash it and hang it up in the locker."

Migliaccio always carries extras just in case players forget. "Sometimes, guys will take their uniform belt off, hang it on a hook in their locker, and forget about it," he said. "I'll go around and look to make sure, but sometimes they forget. That's one of the little things. You can get to a city, and 12 guys forgot their belt. I have extras, but I'd rather they use their own."

When the season ends, Migliaccio and equipment manager Jason Shawger do a thorough inventory of the equipment in house and begin planning for the next year. "A lot of times, you can carry uniforms over from one season to the next," Migliaccio said. "As players change, you need to work with PR departments to assign players numbers. I can get their uniform information from their former team or by calling Majestic because they have those things on file. So we have to get stuff ordered for returning guys and new guys. We get their sizes, place their bat orders, and get things ready for spring training."

For some spring training is a relaxed, leisurely time. For the clubhouse staff, though, it can be hectic. "In spring training you are doing a lot of the same things as you would during the regular season, but you have twice as many players," he said. "We'll have 55 players and extra coaches around. So there are more people to clothe, feed and more equipment to provide."

Years ago, players would come to camp a little heavy and might need smaller pants at the end of camp than they did at the beginning. "Now players come down in shape. They play 30 games, and more services are required. Sometimes, there are two games in a day. It is a lot more intense than it used to be."

Migliaccio and his staff prepare for spring training by packing the equipment trucks in January and then coming down for fantasy camp, where they provide the lawyers, dentists, teachers, and machinists with the same level of service as the big leaguers. As is the case during the season, guys at fantasy camp learn that what happens in the clubhouse stays in the clubhouse.

"It's kind of a different world," Migliaccio said. "In some ways players have changed. They're more quiet now. They spend more time on their phones and their laptops than they do getting on each other like the old days. With social media and the Internet, guys have to be more careful away from the ballpark than they used to. But the game really hasn't changed. My job is to just support the players and make sure they're ready to play."

One of the most common questions Migliaccio is asked: how many baseballs do you go through in a game? The answer: it varies from night to night. "We start with about six dozen in the bag, and usually you add into that," Migliaccio said. "The ballboy who handles them has to keep track. If he's getting low, he lets us know, and we'll bring down more to fill the bag. We usually go through about eight dozen a game. That's about average."

Before each game the number of balls can depend on the pitcher, the amount of foul balls, and—for lack of a better term—luck. The balls are rubbed with "mud," which takes the shine off the balls and allows pitchers and fielders to get a firmer grip. Mud is actually Lena Blackburne Baseball Rubbing Mud, and big league teams have cases of it on hand.

Years ago, the plate umpire was charged with rubbing the baseballs. Over time, the duty was passed on to clubhouse attendants in the umpire's room. There are times when you'll find Brewers bullpen coach Marcus Hanel, whose hands are big enough to hold seven baseballs, rubbing up the balls. "Umpires don't do it any more," Migliaccio said.

The Brewers get a shipment of baseballs every month. "Between practice and games, I think we go through 2,000 or 2,200 dozen," Migliaccio said. "That's a lot of balls." When the Brewers leave for a road trip, they'll bring along two or three big ball bags, each holding between 10 and 12 dozen balls. "When we get to each city, we exchange balls," Migliaccio said. "You get two cases a day. If you go into a town for three days, you get six cases to work with. That usually covers it. There are six dozen balls in a case. We get six cases. That covers bullpen sessions, batting practice, and everything else. Whatever you don't use, you just take with you.

Usually at the end, you have balls left. By sharing with other teams, it cuts back on the number of baseballs you have to pack up. They take up a lot of room. If we went on a 10-day trip, we'd have to bring 10 or 20 cases of balls or something stupid like that."

Fans who are lucky enough to attend batting practice on the road might not realize that the balls are different between batting practice and the games. "Rawlings offers a training ball that is a little less costly,"

Migliaccio said. "The game balls are more premiere. They go through more of an inspection process. They can be rejected, and a lot of those rejects are used for batting cages. You can use them for BP. Then there is a training ball, which is tailored more for pitching machines and soft-toss hitting drills and things like that. You can save a little money by buying those."

At one point in the late 1990s, Rawlings changed the color of the baseball box from green to black. Don "Skid" Rowe, the Brewers' somewhat eccentric pitching coach at the time, had a theory. "The black box balls are juiced," Rowe said. "They feel harder and they go farther."

Rowe's theory was neither proven, but he was passionate about it, and home runs did seem to spike after the change.

Players treat their bats like carpenters treat a hammer, or virtuosos treat a prized violin—as tools of the trade. Like most things in baseball, bats are different today than they were even a few years ago. "There used to be two main companies: Louisville Slugger and Adirondack," Migliaccio said. "Now I think there are 32 or 33 licensed bat companies that you can order from or that players can choose from. Marucci has come a long way. Rawlings is making a push to come back into things. Louisville has been a mainstay and remains pretty solid in business. There is the Sam Bat, which Ryan Braun uses. The other ones, you get a few guys here and there. It kind of goes in trends with the team. You get a few players using, say, a Zinger bat. You might get a little wave of guys that will try that company."

The price of a bat varies by company, model, and wood. Maple bats can run $85 to $90 per bat. Ash is a bit cheaper at about $50 per bat. Most players settle on one bat model and stick with it. Others try different things at various points in their career. When I played, we were a little less exacting than they are today. In fact we used to have a community bat bag. Each guy put a few bats in, and it was full. Now each player has his own personal bat bag that can carry about a dozen bats on the road.

Braun uses a Sam Bat model KB1 (which is now an RB8 signature model). He's used that eight of the nine years he's been with the Brewers. He is particular about the model, sometimes re-weighing bats to make sure they meet his specs. Braun uses a large bat relative to other players.

How does a player pick a bat? "A lot of it is about feel," Migliaccio said. "What feels good to you? What feels good to you might not feel good to me. Some guys swing a heavier bat; other guys feel good with a 30-ounce bat rather than a 34-ounce bat. It's all what feels good to you. Some guys are more particular with their bats to the point where they want to weigh them. With Braun we kind of have developed a routine and we re-weigh them.

"Roland Hernandez [founder of RockBats, a purveyor of maple bats] was part of the group that did the early studies on the slope of the grain when they tried to cut back on the two-piece fractures of bats going into the stands and hurting people. He is a wood scientist and he was looking for the grain and the right sound. We re-weighed them and started to grade them out ourselves with a grading caliper. We were looking for the grain and listening for the right sound. Braun would pick the best bats out of the dozen or so that came out. The maple—because it's such a dense wood—you can look at a bat and think it's solid, and then a guy takes it up to the plate, and it explodes. When you look inside the bat, if the grain goes down the middle, it can have more of an angle or a slope and they can break. Major League Baseball has put in guidelines that manufacturers have to follow. Each bat has to meet a certain slope of grain, and they are catalogued with an ID number when they go through the process. They've cut down on multiple fractured bats in games since they put those rules in place. Broken bats are a lot less common now."

Many players find a bat they like and stick with it for their entire career. Robin Yount used a Louisville Slugger P72 with pine tar slathered high up the handle. "Robin didn't use more than three or four dozen bats a year, and he was playing every day," Migliaccio said. "There is something to be said with the consistency of the player. Guys that are better players don't break as many bats. We had an outfielder in the 1980s, Mark Brouhard, who seemed like he could break six bats in an afternoon of batting practice. Rob Deer was another guy who broke a lot of bats. He would change daily sometimes. He'd be trying different things, and I couldn't get them fast enough. By the time I put an order in, he'd have already gone to something else. He could go through 10 or 12 dozen in a season, easy."

Early in his career with the Brewers, second baseman Rickie Weeks experimented with several bats. "When Rickie first came up, he had a bat with a huge handle and he had a few wrist problems, so they tried to get him to taper that handle down," Migliaccio said. "We went through a lot of samples, so he ended up having quite a few bats. It was trial and error getting him to a point where he could have a comfortable bat where he felt good and the medical staff felt it was something he could swing without hurting himself."

When a bat breaks, they are taken to the authentication department and are often taken to the marketing or community relations departments for projects. Some may get sold at the clubhouse store, too.

Injuries are part of baseball, too. When one player goes on the disabled list, he's usually replaced by someone from the minor leagues. The new player needs a jersey. "When we travel throughout the year, part of our extra equipment stock is carrying blank jerseys and numbers, everything you need to make a jersey," Migliaccio said. "In each city we have a reciprocal relationship with the visiting clubhouse staff that take care of us. They have a seamstress on hand that they work with, so if we get into a city late at night and someone calls and says, 'We're bringing up so-and-so,' I can get to the park early that morning, pull out everything I need, call our contact, and have them come out and put a jersey together within just a couple of hours. That's one great thing about Majestic Athletic being the licensee and having all of the team for uniforms—they have a good bank of knowledge as to everyone's sizes."

In 2008 the Brewers were exploring a trade for lefty CC Sabathia. With the July 4 holiday approaching, Migliaccio knew that Majestic's offices would be shut down for the holiday, so he rolled the dice and ordered uniforms to Sabathia's size and specifications ahead of time. "If it didn't go down, it would have been a collector's item," he said. "Fortunately, it worked out."

When a veteran player joins a team—either through trade or free agency—he often requests a specific number. There are stories of players trading Rolex watches, automobiles, or Caribbean cruises for preferred numbers, but those cases are rare. "A lot of it is just respect for the game," Migliaccio said. "If it's a younger guy, they usually understand. It's common courtesy. A lot of times, I'll call the player and ask if they'll change. Sometimes players work it out themselves. When Trevor Hoffman came over from San Diego, there isn't a lot of doubt you're going to give him No. 51."

One of Migliaccio's favorite jersey stories involved No. 52. "We acquired Mike Boddicker, a right-handed pitcher, from Baltimore during a road trip in 1993, and he was wearing No. 52 with the Orioles," he said. "We had a pitcher, Carlos Maldonado, who had that number. We decided to give Maldonado No. 50. We did that on the road. When we got home at the end of a 10-day trip, it slips your mind that you have to switch to the home jersey. Sure enough, we got to Milwaukee, and the game was about to start, and Maldonado came to me in a No. 52 jersey and said, 'Hey, Papi. What am I supposed to do?' I told him to put his jacket on and go out to the bullpen. I called my local guys and said, 'I need a jersey right now.' They came down and made a jersey with the right name and number, and I got it out to the bullpen by the fifth inning—just in case Maldonado got into the game. It was funny. As hard as you try, those things can happen."

Clubhouse Pranks

Abig league clubhouse is a multi-purpose facility. First and foremost, it's an office, a workplace. The business of playing baseball is transacted within the walls. It's also a health club, restaurant, lounge, and a place to change clothes and shower. If your team is winning, it can feel like a magical place that you can't wait to visit. If your team is losing, it can feel like a prison camp.

And at times, it feels like a seventh-grade locker room.

When you get a bunch of guys together with a lot of free time on their hands—especially in a competitive and testosterone-fueled environment—you are going to have some hijinks. It goes beyond blowing a bubble and putting the gum on the top of an unsuspecting teammate's cap. I've seen card games erupt into scuffles. I've seen clothing shredded and shoes nailed to the floor. One of our favorite tricks was to take a guy's street clothes into the shower, saturate them with water, and then put them in a chest freezer that they kept in the training room. A lot of times, clothes were just hidden. Brewers pitcher Willie Mueller, a native of West Bend, Wisconsin, once emerged from the shower to find his pants missing. He had to go back to the hotel wearing a sport coat, dress shirt, and baseball pants.

The gags are a mix of highbrow—phony letters from fans (or their lawyers)—to bottom of the barrel (throwing a bucket of water on someone who is using a bathroom stall). Sometimes, prankers will go for the long haul. The Brewers media guide came out, and Mark Kiefer's bio included an interesting tidbit in the miscellaneous section: "Once swam from San Francisco to Alcatraz Island in three hours." When reporters approached Kiefer about his "feat" during spring training, he responded with a confused look and said, "I don't know what you're talking about."

Kiefer had been had. The previous September, Brewers media relations director Jon Greenberg had given players a questionnaire to fill out. Kiefer left his unattended, and knuckleballer Steve Sparks picked it up and took some creative license. For the record the distance between Alcatraz and Aquatic Park in the Bay of San Francisco is about 1.25 miles, and experienced swimmers can do it in about 40 minutes.

Not all jokes are that cerebral. There was a time when the "hot foot" was all the rage. Whether in the dugout or in the clubhouse, guys would sneak up to an unsuspecting teammate and light his shoelaces on fire. You would see guys crawling on their bellies, under the dugout bench in order to pull this one off. I was caught on TV crawling under the bench in Kansas City to light up Bert Blyleven when we were teammates with the Angels. The Brewers were lighting so many laces on fire that manager George Bamberger called a team meeting. "All right guys, fun is fun," Bamberger said, mixing in a few of his favorite Bronx-flavored curse words. "But these hot foots have got to stop." As Bamberger spoke, an unnamed player—it may have been Rick Cerone—lit his laces on fire, ending the meeting.

At some point the hot foot became boring and fell out of favor. During one camp in Sun City, Arizona, Charlie Moore poured a puddle of rubbing alcohol in front of Gorman Thomas' locker and waited awhile before walking by and casually tossing a match, which created a small bonfire. Nobody batted an eye.

A lot of times, guys will be the subject of a prank and then get revenge on the practical joker later. That had to be the case in the mid-1980s, when a group of pitchers teamed up to "get" Bob McClure, who was pretty good with a joke. One hot, sticky Sunday morning, he came in after a pretty rough Saturday night and decided he wasn't really up to shagging fly balls during batting practice. At that time the bullpens were out in right-center field. The home bullpen was in front, and in the back was the visiting bullpen located right under the old Winston sign at the bottom of the scoreboard. In that area there was an old, cinder block building with no ventilation, no nothing. It's where the bathroom was located.

McClure decided to go and hide in the bullpen and rest until BP was over. Reggie Cleveland, Jerry Augustine, Bob Galasso, and Billy Castro found out he was having a rough morning and got creative. There was a giant flagpole in right-center that had a big, long rope on it. Since the door to the bathroom opened inward, the guys tied the flagpole rope to the door knob—essentially locking McClure in the bathroom with no way to get out. Near the end of batting practice, McClure woke up and tried to get out. "I swear it was 115 degrees inside, like a hot box," McClure recalled later. "I was in there for 15 minutes, yanking so hard on the door the flagpole almost bent in half. It looked like I had a big old bass on the end of that pole." The entire team cracked up. Finally, someone from the grounds crew let him out, and he went to the clubhouse soaked with sweat and mad as hell. He didn't say anything, though, and I'm sure he probably got revenge on his tormentors. But that was a funny morning.

Spring training is often the prime time for pranks. One of the staples in a baseball clubhouse is the "three-man lift." It starts with two or more veteran players arguing—usually in front of a group of rookies—about how strong they are and how much weight they can lift.

At a certain point, someone will suggest a three-man lift to settle the argument. What happens then is three players—almost always rookies— lie on their backs next to each other on the ground and lock arms and legs. The "strong man" is supposed to straddle the middle player, who is almost always the newbie, and try to lift him up by his midsection and somehow get all three players off the ground. It would be a deadlift of about 600 or more pounds, but it never comes to that. Once the players are on the ground and the lifter is done with his hype moves, he will duck out of the way, and the player in the middle, pinned by a teammate on either side, is then doused with water, Gatorade, baby powder, Cruex, Icy Hot, and any other substance available in the clubhouse.

The Brewers once got catcher Bobby Hughes on the three-man lift. Bobby was a second-round draft pick from USC in his first big league camp and he was a weightlifter, so he got sucked into the strong man argument quickly and was doused. The following year a couple veterans told Bobby he was no longer a rookie and invited him to take part in the three-man lift—only this time he was invited to be on the outside. He was ostensibly in on the joke. At least it *seemed* that way. Once the dousing started, it was Hughes who got it again.

Hearing a story like that may make people wonder how can management allow behavior like that. But sometimes management is actually in on the joke. One of baseball's time-honored traditions is to haze a first-year batboy early in his tenure. A manager, coach, player, or even another batboy will send the unsuspecting newbie on an impossible errand like, "Go get me a box of curveballs, kid. Ask the pitching coach where they are," or "Run down to the clubhouse and ask the trainer for a bucket of steam," or "Ask the hitting coach for the keys to the batter's box We can't start batting practice without them."

Now these might sound like silly orders, but new batboys are always eager to please and don't always question authority. The idea is to keep the kid running from person to person. "I don't know where that item is, son, but if you go ask [insert person's name], he'll be able to help you." I've seen this get as far as ownership levels. A nervous batboy once asked Bud Selig for the keys to the batter's box. He went along, sending the kid to find general manager Harry Dalton.

In the early days of Miller Park, the Brewers had a slugging first baseman, Richie Sexson. He was 6'8" and hit some long homers. During batting practice Sexson hit a ball that broke a window at Friday's Front Row Sports Grill in left field. Leftfielder Geoff Jenkins, Sexson's teammate and closest friend, razzed him mercilessly about having to pay for the window. A day or two later, general manager Dean Taylor dropped a fake invoice on the chair in front of Sexson's locker. Sexson read it and was simultaneously incredulous and livid. The letter said that he had to pay for the replacement window and that $3,200 would be withheld from his next paycheck.

Sexson showed his teammates, including Jenkins, the letter just as Taylor, who initiated the whole gag, walked into the clubhouse and started a heated argument. Finally, Taylor yelled, "Just pay for the window!" and walked out. On his way out, Taylor took a long look at Jenkins. "His mouth was open, and his eyes were the size of saucers," Taylor said. The first baseman and GM had set the left fielder up. After exiting, Taylor returned, and everybody— including Jenkins—got a big laugh.

Being able to laugh at yourself is a necessary survival skill in a big-league clubhouse.

During the Brewers' playoff run in 2011, Ryan Braun stumbled rounding third on what would have been an inside-the-park home run. He got to third base, and coach Eddie Sedar was waving him around and Braunie got so excited that he just lost control, stumbled, and did a face-plant between third and home. He was tagged out, which was bad, but he drove in a run, and the Brewers won the game so everybody laughed about it.

That was just the beginning.

The next day pitchers Yovani Gallardo and Shaun Marcum—with help from bullpen catcher Marcus Hanel—created a crime scene of sorts. Using athletic tape they made three figures of Braun out on the field. The first, affixed to a protective screen in front of third base, depicted Braun running with his right arm up in the air. The second depicted Braun face-down between third base and home plate. The third, positioned about two-thirds of the way toward the plate, depicted Braun on his side. All the silhouettes had Braun's uniform number (8) on them. The trio even went so far as to tape a bat in front of the first prone figure, which represented a kind of speed bump. The entire thing looked like an episode of *CSI: Milwaukee*. The Brewers didn't have batting practice on the field that day, so Braun didn't get to see his teammate's handiwork. "Even if he doesn't see it, we can still laugh," third baseman Casey McGehee said.

For a guy whose potential homer turned into an RBI triple (he was tagged out), Braun took the ribbing in stride. "The further I get away

Yovani Gallardo is not only a great pitcher, but also a great prankster, as evidenced by the athletic tape crime scene he created to poke fun at Ryan Braun's base-path spill. *(Courtesy: David Bernacchi)*

from it, the funnier it becomes," he said, the next day. When the play was replayed on *SportsCenter* and other highlight shows, Braun received dozens of texts from friends. One of them, his neighbor and NBA star Reggie Miller, was at the game and went to dinner with Braun afterward. "He was laughing about it," Braun said of Miller.

When a player crashes into a wall, a lot of times players also will make the outline of the body with tape. Things like that can relieve the tension that builds up during a season.

Every once in a while, when the Brewers are in a losing streak, Bob Uecker will pull out a secret weapon. It's a tape made by a sound effects company of a man having an explosive—and exceedingly long—bowel movement. Sophomoric? Yes. But it gets guys laughing so hard that a couple of losses or a 0-for-12 streak doesn't seem so daunting.

Bullpen guys have their own traditions and rhythms. A few years ago, Seth McClung, a Brewers reliever, was injured and did not accompany the team on a trip to the West Coast. With free time on his hands, McClung went to Miller Park and decorated the bullpen bathroom. He put posters there with rugs and magazines and even a candle, which he claimed was to combat Todd Coffey's mid-game visits to the bathroom. He put in a refrigerator to keep Gatorade cold. And he tried to personalize items for each member of the bullpen. Few players enjoyed being part of the Brewers' family than McClung.

You may have noticed that many of these pranks—aside from the occasional dugout hotfoot—take place away from the game. For the nine innings, players are generally pretty serious. But there are times when things are called for. On July 4, 2015, Brewers center fielder Carlos Gomez left a gift for his counterpart Billy Hamilton. As the bottom of the third inning ended, Gomez left a pile of gum and a note for Hamilton that read, "I see you dropped all your gum so I brought you some more." TV cameras captured Gomez leaving the gum, Hamilton finding it, and both men laughing as a result.

It's not always losing teams that need a boost. You see nowadays that winning players who do walk-off interviews with sideline reporters immediately after the game are often besieged by teammates pouring water, Gatorade, sunflower seeds, gum, and shaving cream pies (which burn the eyes). It was funny for a while, but I really think that ship has sailed. I was watching a game one time and players in Anaheim doused a teammate with chocolate syrup. I don't think that's necessary, and it's not just because I work in broadcasting and hate to see my colleagues get their clothes ruined. It just seems a bit tired to me unless you just won a playoff game.

The Training Room

Early in my big league career, I did just about anything I could to avoid going into the training room. It was a place to socialize, grab an aspirin for a headache, and catch up on the latest jokes and gossip.

After a particularly tough night, some guys found the training table offered a good place to catch a nap. What I didn't want to do was let people know that I was injured. There was a lot of peer pressure—particularly from veteran players—to keep minor aches and pains quiet. The "rub a little dirt on it" mentality permeated much of the game at that time. Significant injuries, of course, were an exception. But guys who spent time in the training room with minor aches were subject to catcalls, ridicule, and remarks like, "You can't make the club in the tub."

Times have definitely changed. These days the training room in a big league clubhouse—and even some of the newer minor league clubhouses—resemble high-tech medical clinics.

Many players visit the training room several times a day—often for hours at a time to stretch, rehab, ice, exercise, get massage therapy, or heat a muscle. There is no stigma to being in the training room. In fact, it would be silly for a player not to avail himself of the resources at hand.

Need a massage? Most teams employ at least one therapist. Need to exercise a problem area? They can help. The entire training room experience has evolved from a "don't ask, don't tell" mind-set to "get as much help as you can." One thing, however, hasn't changed: rookies are expected to arrive early, so they can get treatment and make way for later arriving veterans.

Clubs used to employ a single trainer, and then assistant trainers were added to help. Today, the medical departments are robust. Here is a look at the Brewers' medical roster.

Roger Caplinger, who started with the Brewers organization as a trainer in the Rookie League more than 25 years ago, worked his way up through the ranks and is now director of medical operations. Caplinger is in charge of athletic training, strength, conditioning, and the medical staff for all levels of the organization. He is in charge of budgeting, worker's compensation, and implementing things like emergency response teams at Miller Park.

Dan Wright, the head athletic trainer, was Caplinger's assistant for 10 seasons. He's also worked with the Cincinnati Reds, Kansas City Royals, and San Francisco Giants. Matt Krug is the team's director of psychological services. With a doctorate in counseling psychology from Marquette University, Krug has worked at IMG Academies in Bradenton, Florida, and has been with the team five years. Dave Yeager is the assistant athletic trainer, helping Wright split the duties. Yeager also spent time with Double A Huntsville. Josh Seligman is the Brewers' strength and conditioning specialist. He came to Milwaukee in 2011 after spending seven years as a minor league coordinator and rehab specialist for the Miami Marlins. Kevan Creighton assists Wright as an athletic trainer and works as a massage therapist. Creighton, who began his Brewers career as an intern in 2008, was a sprinter and jumper in college at the University of Wisconsin-Milwaukee.

In order to get a better handle on the way the training room operates, I spoke with Wright, who in 2016 will enter his 15th season with the club and his fifth as head athletic trainer.

Bill Schroeder: When I played we had one or two trainers, and he might have a guy who tagged along, taping ankles. Now, you have a whole team. Why did that change?

Dan Wright: We essentially needed to increase our hands-on coverage—especially on the road—because the demands over the last five-plus years, the need for player care, and the intensity of player care have increased.

BS: Why is the home/road thing important?

DW: We evened the playing field in terms of the level of care both home and away. We used to have a lot of hands at home and a couple hands on the road. Now we're able to even that out a little bit. It gives us a continuum of player care on the road. That's really important.

BS: How are players different today than a generation ago or even a few years ago? Why are they more demanding now?

DW: The players have more expectation and exposure to the types of therapies and different types of things out there that give them an advantage in injury prevention and performance enhancements. The information available to guys, whether it's via social media, Internet, through their agents, people who know people, other players or any source— there is just a continually growing level of things out there that guys like to use or look into to try to help themselves…The economics for sure have changed. I think that has created kind of a self-imposed change in their own expectations. The game is the same. The game hasn't changed. But the dressing around it certainly has.

BS: What are the qualifications to be an athletic trainer?

DW: Well, I stayed at a Holiday Inn Express last night…Actually, it's pretty standard across the board. Whether you are in pro baseball or a clinical or school situation, all athletic trainers have to be certified by the National Board of Athletic Trainers Association. We all pass a certification board. In order to sit for that board, you used to need a minimum of a bachelor's degree. Now it's become a minimum of a master's degree. All of us on our staff have a master's degree. We tend to be an educated bunch.

In addition to being certified, just like any other allied health care professional like a physical therapist or occupational therapist, we have to maintain continuing education units. The bottom line is you have to have an education based with the degrees I mentioned. In baseball, it's basically moving up the ladder based on the experience and connections you have.

BS: What is spring training like for the medical staff?

DW: There are a couple major directions we look into. For starters we're closing out the offseason. We follow these guys throughout the course of the offseason. The majority of that contact is through phone, email, and texting. Our guys are spread all over the country and the world. The offseason programs, whether they be strength maintenance, conditioning programs, rehabilitative programs, or are working with a therapist in our country or abroad, we maintain those contacts to see where guys are or if they have new issues coming up or if they're dealing with old issues from prior seasons.

BS: Do you have to struggle to contact players in the winter, or do they reach out to you?

DW: It's not unusual for me to get calls to solve a problem. Someone who is in the Dominican Republic, who has an internal issue that needs to be taken care of, may call. It can be anything. Basically, we try to assure that guys come to spring training ready to go. Our pitchers are expected to be ready to step on the mound and start throwing sides (side sessions) with our pitching coaches, and our position players are stepping into the box hitting and doing defensive work right out of the chute. They have to be ready to go when the bell rings.

BS: How do you keep guys honest? What if a guy says he's been working out, and he's actually been eating cheeseburgers and pizza all winter?

DW: With guys spread out, we have ways to reach out. We can do video things, Skype, and things like that. Those are usually situations where we have our doubts. I've gone to Florida a couple times in the past to check on players. I've gone to Texas, Louisiana…just to make sure that guys didn't have issues with physical therapy in post-surgical situations. It's one thing to hear a player tell you that they're in such and such a state and at a particular weight, but it's another thing to actually go see that player and see where they are. Sometimes, they don't match up. In the end when it comes to spring training, we know who does and who doesn't. You don't want to get to that point to find out when camp opens.

BS: What's the most important part of spring training for the medical staff?

DW: Our biggest production is at the beginning when we have our spring training physicals. For years we have a very comprehensive spring training physical screening process. It covers all orthopedic issues, internal issues, eye check, all down the line. We do a number of different things to make sure guys are healthy and that any ortho issues that existed are not a problem anymore. We are talking to over 50 guys, and it takes a great deal of time and precision.

BS: Is it harder with players who come from other teams?

DW: With new arms, pitchers that come into camp—whether that be a new free agent or whether it be a minor league pitcher up from our system—if it's their first time in our camp, they're going to get a baseline MRI for their shoulder or elbow so we have something to refer to in the future.

BS: This sounds pretty complex.

DW: It takes a great deal of planning. We're running anywhere from 55 to 65 physicals, depending on the year. It's a very individualized process and it takes an entire day to go through and basically another day to go through the information and sift out where we have problems.

All the information is gathered in a report and given to the front office. If there are any red flags, we have a grading system where we give the front office an ability to look at a player and say, "This player is at this particular risk level." They can make decisions on what they want to do moving forward.

BS: Let's shift gears a bit and talk about game situations. What is it like when you have to run on the field to treat a player who gets hit in the head by a pitch?

DW: Any time you have to go out on the field, there is a management—crisis management that happens right at the first contact. As the athletic trainer, for me when things get serious, that's when I go into calm mode. You have to keep a level of sanity. Usually, the player is mad. There may also be a level of fear because of the unknown. You have to calm that player down. Once you get to a level where you can communicate, you have to do an assessment on the field. With a head or neck injury, you go through and manage that crisis. You have to assess the level of consciousness, make sure the player is conscious. You see what their level of communication is, if they are lucid. Can they talk to you? Can they understand what you're saying to them? Then you're scanning to see what the injury is. Was it a ball hitting the helmet? A ball hitting the face? Could there be head or neck issues. Once we see a guy is conscious and responsive to us, there is no blunt trauma, once you assess those things and you're past those things, you start going through the cognitive process. There are a number of levels in concussive exams that you go through. It's really standard.

BS: What are you asking a player in that situation? What are you looking for?

DW: After the initial exam, we check vision, check for nausea, ringing in the ears. Is there fluid coming from the ears or nose? The first thing I ask a player is, "Can you hear me?" Then I'll say, "What did you feel? What happened?" I see if he can recount the memory.

Sometimes they don't respond due to shock. When they respond we ask things like "Can you feel your fingers?" and "Do you have any numbing or tingling in lower extremities. Can you turn your neck? We start going through upper extremity strength and sensation exams pretty quickly to make sure everything is connected. If they pass that and can tell me what happened—the day, the score, the count—we'll sit them up, and go through another round of tests and questions.

We're always looking for outward signs of trauma. Once a guy moves, you may see something that you didn't see before. If everything seems okay, we'll have the player stand up and go through it again. So we test three times—the first position, sitting, and standing—depending on the trauma. Once Rickie Weeks got hit in the face and would not come out of the game. There was no diagnosed concussion, and he was able to take the trauma. Other guys may be affected differently. Each case is different. If there is any doubt whatsoever, we simply take them out of the game.

BS: Do you ever feel pressure from umpires, managers, or even players to hurry things up?

DW: The rules have changed. The umpires are directed to make sure everybody stays out of our way and that there is no rush. We have as much time as we want, and it really helps us out a lot. There is no sense that we have anybody breathing down our neck to make a potentially life-altering decision. If we take a player inside, we have doctors on hand and we have exams that they'll go through.

BS: How do you go about informing the front office and the broadcasters?

DW: One of the first things I'll do is text (assistant general manager) Gord Ash to give him the initial impression. I'll say, "We're taking a player out because possible concussive event," or, "We're taking player out because of a left leg injury or shoulder tightness," whatever the basic description may be just so they can feed you guys information and give you an idea what is going on. After we have had time to go through a deeper assessment of what an injury is or what other diagnostics may be necessary, I'll call Gord and give him the details of what we think it is what the plan is and what we need to move forward.

BS: Are there situations where players want to play against medical advice?

DW: We do listen to players, but at the same time, we have to balance what the greater good is for the club. There have been times when we have weighed based on a player's opinion or their wish. Fortunately, with our club we have not just a manager but a front office that has been very good in the past, allowing us to and entrusting our ability to make an assessment and a prediction on where a particular injury may go.

BS: Traumatic injuries can happen, but that's not every night. What's a normal day like in the training room?

DW: It's a little different on the road than at home, but let's say we have a home night game. Our day—just by virtue of the way the game is—is skewed forward a little bit. I tend to wake up a little later in the morning around 9:00 or 9:30 AM. We will go to the ballpark between 12:30 to 1:00 PM for a 7:10 PM game. Once we get there, we all have certain things we do just to get the day started administratively or facility-wise to get things prepped for the players coming in. Players typically start coming in, some as early as 1:30 PM, but on average they arrive between 2:00 and 3:30 PM based upon the day and who they are and what their role is with the club.

We're a pretty hands-on medical staff. We do a tremendous amount of hands-on work with guys. There are a couple reasons for that. One, it gives us a day-to-day feel, whether we're stretching a pitcher or we are able to monitor what that guy's range is. Or, if it's strength work, we get a feel with respect to where they are. It goes back to spring training preparation. We may see certain deficits that we know we have to address. A guy may not have a particular complaint, but we may notice that it's different from the past or in a range that we know from research will put a guy at risk. We'll constantly be doing things to counteract those deficits.

We also do monthly reassessments with our pitchers and range of motion. We're constantly looking at those numbers and doing things to make sure that those things are addressed. You get up to the point where guys get ready to go on the field for early work at 3:00 PM. We may have guys that—if we have someone who is rehabilitating—we may go out and do a throwing program, or if it is a lower-body issue, we may do that at our time. At around 4:10 PM, the team will go out for their stretch and warm-up and throwing and prep for batting practice. During batting practice our athletic trainers will typically be out there for that time.

BS: I'm always amazed more guys don't get hurt during batting practice.

DW: It looks like controlled chaos. There are a lot of moving parts. We take it for granted because we understand what is going on. Things can happen. They have happened. We typically want to cover that with one of us. We'll get through our batting practice and come back to the clubhouse, where players will get a pregame meal and we go into prep mode. You've got guys coming in to get some warm-up-type activity, some movement-prep type things to get them ready to go for the game. Some guys may do some taping. Some guys just do their own deal with that. We're usually getting our starting pitcher ready to go for the game.

BS: Do pitchers go through similar routines or are they all different?

DW: Each guy has some form of active warm-up. After the active warm-up, we're doing some sort of manual muscle work to get them stretched to get them warmed up. Once they've done that, they've got some of their own little things that they do: movement prep, active warm-up, active range of motion—whether it's arm, hips, or lower leg stuff. That's the time that we do that. At that point we get ready for the game. We cover the game just like we do batting practice. It may look like we're just standing there, chewing some sunflower seeds, and talking to guys, but you have to understand that from our perspective and for me, personally, you have to be prepared to go from zero to 90 at any given second. Anything can happen. Guys can get hurt. People get hit by pitches. There are collisions on the base path, collisions in the outfield, collisions with walls.

BS: Are there any players you've worked with who stand out in terms of preparation?

DW: Hoffy (Trevor Hoffman) was in the upper echelon of a guy who is dedicated and professional and very serious about what he did on a daily basis to physically and mentally prepare for the game. He went into every day with the belief that *I'm going to pitch today.* His prep would start an hour before the game. His workout stuff would occur even before that. His prep work would start anywhere from an hour before the game and go into the third inning or so, and it's not all hands-on stuff with us, but things he would do to get himself physically and mentally ready to go. He would head down to the pen around the fifth or sixth inning, somewhere around there, and again, just get into the mind-set. After he pitched it would delay the bus on getaway day considerably because of his routine. I don't think anybody got bent out of shape for that. He would come in, and there was a bit of a cooldown period. He'd do his media obligations. We would do an arm-strength maintenance series of some sort, some soft tissue work, a rubdown. It was, without question, an hour or an hour and 10 minutes.

BS: In the old days, guys would just ice their arm and take a shower.

DW: Now, we have a routine for every guy based on a player's use and what his specific needs are. Each pitcher is different, but there is usually some recovery-related work we do.

BS: Do you have a lot of paperwork as part of your job?

DW: We document everything we do every day. Once things start winding down with player care, we will finish up our notes for the day, which we work on through the course of the day. If we're doing treatment with guys, it's written down. If a guy comes in to tape his wrist, we don't do that. Anything that is treatment-related, we do note and document. That last bit of the day is finishing that up. We meet so we don't let anything fall between the cracks, discuss anything new, or anything we need to change if a direction we're going isn't making a difference. We finish the report, we send it, we print it, and that part of the day is done. Then we go grab a bite. We're usually leaving the ballpark at about 11:45 PM or midnight. It's easily a 12-hour day.

BS: Is that a grind?

DW: You get used to it. It's tough to describe, but when you have that 162-game schedule and you've basically got two NBA seasons—a home and away NBA season in the midst of 181 days. When you go 17 days without an off day, it's a challenge. It's a marathon. It's a grind for everybody—for the players, for the clubhouse staff, for the coaching staff, for us, for broadcasters.

COSTLY (AND CRAZY) INJURIES

When you play 162 games in 180 days, nicks and bruises and sprains and muscle pulls are virtually inevitable. Some injuries, though, are more impactful and memorable than others.

Here is a look at some significant—and strange—injuries in Brewers history.

Paul Molitor

As a self-proclaimed "scrawny" kid growing up in St. Paul, Minnesota, Molitor was accident prone and estimates that he broke 10 bones, including his arm when he fell out of a tree.

As a major leaguer, he suffered rib cage problems, hamstring issues, torn ligaments on his ankle, an elbow operation, and more. "The injuries were frustrating certainly, and I couldn't really pinpoint what it was," Molitor said. "I thought that I worked out and took care of myself. Some were more flukish and some were recurring things." Molitor likely missed 500 to 600 games due to injury in his career. Performing at his career average, he could have added nearly 1,000 hits to his total.

Scooter Gennett

Sometimes injuries seem to sweep through the clubhouse like a common cold or stomach virus, moving from one player to another until nobody feels safe...even in the shower. In April of 2015, Brewers second baseman Scooter Gennett was showering after a game at Pittsburgh's PNC Park when he cut his left hand. Gennett, who posted a picture of the injury on his Instagram account, said he was "trying to grab some body wash in the shower and sliced my finger on the bottom of the metal thing that holds the shampoo." The injury required five stitches and earned Gennett a trip to the disabled list.

Jonathan Lucroy

In late May of 2012, Brewers catcher Jonathan Lucroy ended up on the wrong end of a battle with his luggage. While staying at the team hotel in Los Angeles, Lucroy was reaching for a sock underneath his bed when his wife, Sarah, shifted a suitcase, which fell onto Jonathan's hand, causing pain and swelling. When he reported for duty at Dodger Stadium, Lucroy found he could barely grip a bat. Lucroy, who had signed a five-year contract extension during spring training and was hitting .345 at the time of the injury, was diagnosed with a fractured fifth metacarpal bone and ended up having surgery to insert a pin through his knuckle and down through his pinky.

Lucroy's injury capped a month in which the Brewers lost starters Chris Narveson, Alex Gonzalez, and Mat Gamel to injury. As frustrated as he was to be sidelined, Lucroy also became miffed when fans began harassing his wife and questioning the circumstances of the injury via social media. "If they question it, I guess that's fine. That's their right. I really don't care," he said after the surgery. "I have a broken hand. I'm the one who's suffering here. I'm the one that's having a hard time. No one else is besides the team."

Danny Frisella

The Brewers organization was rocked early in 1977 by the death of reliever Danny Frisella, who was killed in a dune buggy crash in Phoenix. Frisella, 30, was a passenger in a dune buggy driven by his close friend, James Wesley, who lost control of the vehicle on a sand dune just a short distance from Frisella's home. The vehicle flipped, and Wesley escaped with minor injuries. The accident turned tragic, though, when the vehicle fell on top of Frisella, and the steel roll bar crushed his skull.

Frisella, who left behind a three-year-old son and a pregnant wife, Pam, had joined the Brewers from the St. Louis Cardinals at the June 15 trading deadline the previous season. After pitching well for the San Diego Padres in 1976, Frisella struggled with control issues with the Cardinals and was shipped to the Brewers, where he worked his way into the closer's job and won teammates over with a tricky forkball and a sharp sense of humor.

Frisella, who struck out 43 batters and chalked up nine saves in 49 innings, was expected to be the Brewers' closer in '77 and beyond. "That is a real shocker," Milwaukee president Bud Selig told the Associated Press. "I'm dumbfounded." First baseman

Catcher Jonathan Lucroy points to the dugout, following his RBI single against the Chicago Cubs months after hurting his hand during an embarrassing incident.

Mike Hegan told *The Sporting News* that Frisella became an important part of the team in a short time. "He was a little off the wall," Hegan said. "He kept guys loose." Manager Alex Grammas told the Associated Press: "We're going to miss his pitching, sure, but we're going to miss having him around, too. He was good to have on the club."

Wes Weger

Most Brewers fans have never heard of Wes Weger, and that anonymity was aided by a freakish injury. A two-time Trans-American Athletic Conference Player of the Year at Stetson University, Weger joined the Brewers organization after being drafted in the 12th round of the 1992 draft. In 1993 Weger was a Texas League All-Star at Double A El Paso, where he hit .298 with five homers and 50 RBIs. He was ranked as one of the top five shortstops in the minor leagues heading into the 1994 season and was enjoying a stint in big league spring training camp when the injury bug hit.

During an exhibition game between the Brewers and Rockies at Compadre Stadium in Chandler, Arizona, a Colorado hitter lost his grip on his bat, which flew into the home dugout. Weger scrambled to get out of the way, but the barrel of the bat hit him on the left ankle.

"At first I thought it was just bruised," Weger told the Orlando Sentinel. "After I got hit, I walked over to get a drink of water and, while it was sore, I didn't think it was hurt that bad."

When the pain persisted, Weger removed himself from the game. While X-rays showed no broken bones, it was still a bad break. Weger suffered from tendinitis and pain that sidelined him for the entire 1994 season. The Brewers had hoped to have Weger ready to play in the big leagues as a utility infielder in the 1995 season. As so often happens, one player's injury led to another player's opportunity.

Mark Loretta, a seventh-round pick out of Northwestern University in 1993, passed Weger on the organizational depth chart and worked his way into a big league call-up in 1995.

Loretta went on to play 15 seasons in the big leagues, including eight in Milwaukee. He was a two-time All-Star (2004, 2006) and now works in San Diego's front office. If it hadn't been for Weger's injury, Loretta may have had to use his business degree from Northwestern to pursue other opportunities.

Ben Sheets

During his eight seasons with the Brewers, Ben Sheets suffered from a handful of maladies that prompted many fans to hang the dreaded "injury prone" label on him. As a rookie in 2001, he spent five weeks on the disabled list with shoulder tendinitis. After a run of three healthy and productive seasons, Sheets signed a four-year, $38.5 million deal—the largest in club history at that point—and a week later suffered a malady that sent media types and fans scrambling for the nearest medical dictionary. During a trip to Los Angeles, Sheets began to feel dizzy and disoriented. He was diagnosed with vestibular neuritis, an inner ear disorder, which affects balance. Most researchers believe vestibular neuritis is caused by a viral infection.

The Brewers weren't sure how Sheets contracted the malady, but it sidelined him for a week and then recurred a year later during a trip in Houston. After battling flu-like symptoms in a 6–1 loss to the Houston Astros on Wednesday night, Sheets was dizzy and vomited on Thursday morning. He called trainer Roger Caplinger and ended up spending the night at The Methodist Hospital in the Texas Medical Center, where he was treated by Astros doctor James Muntz while the rest of the team headed to San Francisco. "The first couple days was straight spinning, then it turned to weak-kneed and disorientation all the time," Sheets told the Milwaukee Journal Sentinel. "Now it's cloudy. Now it's foggy in the head. And there's still some things that make me spin pretty good."

Matt Wise

Ballplayers never hesitate to rip one another in the clubhouse. Guys who are battling weight issues are popular targets, and one of the more common barbs tossed at a portly teammate going through the postgame buffet is "Why don't you mix in a salad?" For Matt Wise that advice was particularly painful. As one of the skinnier players on the team, though, Wise seemed more in need of a cheeseburger, fries, and a chocolate shake than a plate of arugula and kale.

In the 2006 season, a salad ended up forcing him to the sideline. After a Sunday afternoon game in Kansas City, Wise was manipulating a pair of salad tongs and cut his middle finger. The cut required several stitches and limited his ability to throw his change-up, which was his best pitch. "That's what I get for trying to be healthy, I guess," Wise said. "At least it was something in my weight class." Earlier in that season, Wise strained his shoulder when his hand slipped off a rail in the bullpen. In a true display of clubhouse compassion, Marcus Hanel, the Brewers' bullpen catcher, started calling Wise "Bubble Boy" because of the injuries.

Curtis Leskanic

In May of 2000, Curtis Leskanic discovered what appeared to be an ingrown hair on his...well, let's just call it a very private area. He was advised by club medical staff to leave it alone or the results could be disastrous.

Indeed they were.

Leskanic developed an infection that led to cellulitis of the groin area, which was incredibly swollen. He was hospitalized for a time, flushed with antibiotic IVs to battle the infection, and ended up on the disabled list. He was also the butt of numerous clubhouse jokes.

"You guys shouldn't laugh. It's not funny," Leskanic said as he limped past a group of reporters in the clubhouse during his recovery. "Actually, it is funny. If it happened to someone besides me, I'd be laughing."

Bill Spiers

Bill Spiers was ticketed to be the Brewers' starting shortstop in 1992, but a bad back forced him to the sideline just as the team was getting ready to break spring training. That opened the door for Pat Listach. "We were about to break camp and fly to Denver [the Brewers' Class Triple A affiliate at the time], and they called and told me, 'You're in the big leagues,'" Listach said. "They didn't lie to me. They said, 'We don't know how long you're going to be here. We don't know how long Billy is going to be hurt.' But I got off to a good start and fit right in."

Listach became a fixture in first-year skipper Phil Garner's lineup, playing 149 games and hitting .290 with 19 doubles, six triples, 47 RBI, and 54 steals. He was the first player in Brewers history to be named Rookie of the Year by the Baseball Writers Association of America. He edged Kenny Lofton, who stole 66 bases and hit .285 with 15 doubles, eight triples, and 42 RBIs. Listach, though, was derailed by knee problems, which robbed him of his speed. He was out of the big leagues after the 1997 season.

Dale Sveum

Though he'll always hold a place in the hearts of Brewers fans because of his game-winning homer on Easter Sunday in 1987, Dale Sveum also deserves a spot on the "unfortunate injury" roster. A first-round draft pick (25th overall) in 1982, Sveum worked his way to the big leagues as an infielder and put up 25 homers and 95 RBIs as the No. 9 hitter on the 1987 team. The following year, in a September game at Tiger Stadium, Sveum and Darryl Hamilton collided while chasing Scott Lusader's pop-up in short left field. Sveum suffered a broken left tibia.

"I knew the leg was broken," Sveum told The New York Times. "It sounded like a shotgun went off."

Sveum missed the final month of the '88 season and all of '89. Though he stuck around with the Brewers, Philadelphia Phillies, Chicago White Sox, Oakland A's, Seattle Mariners, Pittsburgh Pirates, and New York Yankees, he was never the same. "That changed the course of my life and the course of my career," Sveum said. "I don't dwell on it. I really never have dwelled on it. It's a fact. It's there; I can't change it. It was a crucial time, and it basically ruined my career."

Steve Sparks

He had a cool last name and threw an unusual pitch, but that's not why most Brewers fans remember Steve Sparks. A phonebook took care of that. During spring training in 1994, the Brewers brought a group of motivational speakers dubbed "Radical Reality" to talk to players at Compadre Stadium. As part of the demonstration, a couple of muscle-bound motivators tore thick phonebooks in half to show what inspired people can accomplish.

Sparks, a converted infielder trying to make the big league team for the first time at age 28, grabbed a phonebook and tried to tear it in half. He ended up dislocating his left shoulder.

Though it was his non-throwing shoulder, Sparks had suffered several similar injuries in the past—all of which occurred when his hands were over his head. "I had it halfway ripped apart when my shoulder popped out," he said.

Sparks ended up making the big league club the next season. In 1997 he suffered a more conventional and damaging injury. While covering first base on a potential double-play grounder, Sparks wheeled to make a throw to home plate but stopped his throwing motion. The sudden stop ripped a ligament in his elbow, prompting reconstructive "Tommy John" surgery and ending his season.

David Nilsson

During his years with the Brewers, David Nilsson didn't have to worry about Wisconsin winters. That's because he returned to his native Australia and enjoyed summer Down Under.

While playing winter ball after the 1994 season, Nilsson was stricken with a mosquito-borne virus called Ross River Fever. The disease, which causes symptoms similar to mononucleosis, kept Nilsson on the shelf for the first two months of 1995.

Jeromy Burnitz

Few hitters in Major League Baseball were hotter than Jeromy Burnitz in the summer of 1999. With his confidence high after a second-place showing in the Home Run Derby, Burnitz was intent on carrying the surprising Brewers to heights they hadn't seen in several years.

On July 17, the week after starting in the All-Star Game, where he finished with a double and an RBI, Burnitz stepped in to face Kansas City Royals pitcher Jose Rosado in the bottom of the fourth inning and was plunked on the right hand by a fastball. Burnitz stayed in the game but exited two innings later. X-rays revealed a non-displaced fracture of the fifth metatarsal bone.

The Brewers struggled mightily without Burnitz. Hovering at 44–45 when he went out, they found themselves 52–60 when Phil Garner was fired on August 12. By the time Burnitz returned, they were more than 20 games below .500.

Rollie Fingers

There are many "what if?" questions from the 1982 World Series that haunt Brewers fans, but one stands out: what if Rollie Fingers hadn't gotten hurt? The American League MVP and Cy Young winner in 1981, Fingers helped the Brewers win their first pennant but was sidelined after tearing a muscle in his right forearm on September 2. Though Pete Ladd pitched reasonably well as a replacement down the stretch, many believe Fingers' ability to pitch multiple innings could have turned the tide. "I get that all the time when I come to Milwaukee," Fingers said. "People say, 'I wish you were healthy for the World Series.' I don't know if we would have won, but I would have liked to have had the chance. I think there were a couple of games I could have made a difference. Who knows? I may have messed up. It was tough watching, I'll tell you that."

The Brewers won the opener of the World Series in St. Louis but lost Game 2 when Ladd walked in the winning run in what turned out to be his only appearance in the series. If healthy Fingers almost certainly would have pitched in Game 7, when the Brewers took a 3–1 lead into the seventh inning and saw it disappear in a 6–3 loss. "I'm pretty sure we would have won it all, if Rollie hadn't been hurt," first baseman Cecil Cooper said at a reunion in the early 2000s. "We were short-armed in that series, and Rollie would have made a difference."

Larry Hisle

In 1977 Brewers owner Bud Selig made a splash by signing Oakland third baseman Sal Bando to a free-agent contract. A year later he signed Larry Hisle, who had been a dominant player for Minnesota. In his final season with the Twins, Hisle hit .302 with 28 homers, a league-leading 119 RBIs, 36 doubles, and 21 stolen bases. In his first Milwaukee campaign, Hisle hit 34 homers, drove in 115 runs, and scored 96. He was an All-Star and finished third in MVP voting. Early the next season during a game in Baltimore, Hisle tried to make a throw from the left-field gap and felt a sharp pain in his right shoulder. He had torn his rotator cuff, an injury that effectively ended his career. "People forget what a wonderful player he was," Selig said. "There is no doubt in my mind he could have been an MVP, no doubt. He hit for power. He hit for average. He was just an incredibly talented player."

Joe Inglett

He had a moth in his ear during a game. They had to shine a light in his ear and pick it out with a tweezer.

The Video Revolution

One of the biggest changes in baseball in the past 20 years has been the use of video for player development, scouting, and coaching. Teams have invested millions of dollars and countless hours in an effort to use technology to maximize performance and glean valuable information. Just ask Joe Crawford.

Crawford, known as "Crawdaddy" in the clubhouse, grew up in Ohio, pitched at Kent State University, and was drafted by the New York Mets in the 17th round in 1991. The Boston Red Sox picked him up in the Rule 5 Draft in 1995, but the Mets bought him back a year later.

In 1997 Crawford made it to the big leagues and pitched in 19 games (two starts) for New York. The Mets released him after that season, and he bounced around to other big league camps, including with the Brewers and Arizona Diamondbacks. He pitched in Japan for the Chiba Lotte Marines in 1998–99 and then served as the pitching coach for the Bridgeport Bluefish of the Independent Atlantic League in 2002–03. During his time with New York, Crawford developed a relationship with Jack Zduriencik, who began his career as an area scout and national cross-checker with the Mets. In 1999 Zduriencik was named the Brewers' scouting director.

Crawford was interested in becoming a scout, so he placed a call. (This is another valuable lesson. Baseball works in mysterious ways. The people you meet at any point in your career can help you down the road. That's why you should always be nice to people and never burn a bridge. But your mom and dad already told you that.) Anyway, Crawford called Zduriencik in the fall of 2003 and eventually interviewed for a position as an area scout in the Orlando, Florida, area. After a lunch meeting with Zduriencik and his assistant, Tom Flanagan, Crawford was touring the offices at Miller Park when he bumped into general manager Doug Melvin and assistant GM Gord Ash. "I met with Doug and Gord for about 35 seconds," he said. "A couple days later, Jack informed me he wasn't going to offer me the scouting job. I was bummed. I thought I had a great shot at it. But then he told me to sit tight. His words were, 'I think you might have gotten stolen from me,' but he wouldn't elaborate."

As it turned out, the Brewers were looking to make a transition to using computers and statistics and analytics. They wanted to hire someone who could relate to players, had a college degree, had a scouting eye, and could learn to operate video and computer equipment. Crawford met all those critera, but he also had what turned out to be a pivotal intangible in his back pocket.

"At that time the Brewers didn't have anybody on the staff who was left-handed who could throw batting practice," he said, laughing. "I'm left-handed and I pitched. I fell right into their lap."

For Crawford the transition to life in the clubhouse was easy. He'd played long enough and been around players long enough to fit in easily. The tough part was learning the technology.

"I could program a VCR," Crawford said. "I knew how to make the time stop flashing on the VCR, but that was about the extent of my knowledge, but I wasn't afraid of it. When I got the job, they also hired Karl Mueller, who was a guy who went to school for the new statistical stuff. I was more of the on-field, baseball guy. When they put us together, it was like chocolate and peanut butter. You put us together, and it made a Reese's Cup."

As recently as five years earlier, the Brewers were using a system in which each player had a VHS tape of his at-bats, and another player, generally the starting pitcher from the previous night, was charged with putting that player's tape into a VCR and hitting the record button. Needless to say, it wasn't a perfect setup. When Crawford arrived things were still a tad prehistoric. "We had VCRs with cowboy remotes, the tethered remotes," he said. "Then we really got into the CDs and DVDs. It was annoying and time-consuming, but it had to be done. We had an old system for charting games that they were under contract to use for one more year, so we had to use that."

At about that time, the Brewers and several other clubs began using a system provided by Sydex Sports called B.A.T.S. It was a software program that allowed teams to archive video quickly, cutting hours of tedium off the task. As video became more entrenched, players began to visit Crawford on a regular basis. Soon the video room became a hub of activity just like the training room and the dining room. From the time the clubhouse opens to the time the last player leaves, it's rarely empty. "There is so much to be gleaned from video," Crawford said. "With traditional scouting you might go to a city and watch a guy for a few days. That's important. You need to do that too. But with video you can see every game and every at-bat that a guy has. It has come such a long way. For our players now, it's as much a part of their day as batting practice and stretching and everything else."

When teams first started utilizing video, players were looking for specific things. "A lot of times, guys would come back after striking out and they'd watch the pitch and see that the umpire had totally screwed them," Crawford said. "They'd go back to the dugout and say, 'That was a ball! I told you!' You don't see that much anymore. Players are so computer-savvy. The young guys aren't intimidated by it. They use it most of the time the right way."

The integration of video and analytics rankled some of the old guard in the scouting profession, but many have come to accept that the new age is here to stay. "It's not going to go backward," Crawford said. "There is so much information available, but you've got to filter through it and use the right stuff. People differ on what is and what is not the right stuff. My job is to provide everything, give my opinion if it's asked."

For Crawford a normal day starts when he arrives in the video room at about 10:00 AM.

"If we're playing a team in a series, that's not the team I'm generally working on," he said. "I'm already working a road trip ahead. I start loading hard drives that I'll take on the road with me. I like to do that before players and coaches show up because that's when I have the most computers available. I also get things ready for the coaches' scouting meetings and anything else that might be needed. Eddie Sedar might want to look at a relief pitcher's pickoff move. We can call it up and see if he does anything to give away his throws to first."

The amount of archived information players and coaches can access is almost staggering. The Brewers have access to literally every pitch thrown in every game in the major leagues in a season. "It goes all the way back to 2009," Crawford said. "It will blow your mind—the things you can search for. The guys upstairs use information for writing scouting reports. We use it to show players and coaches. The key is that we can filter the information. If we're playing the Cardinals, we can say, 'Let me see all the pitches that Adam Wainwright throws when he's behind in the count with runners in scoring position.' We may see that in that situation he goes to the curveball 80 percent of the time. That's what the guys in scouting hammer when they write their reports. You see tendencies. In my video room, players can sit down and say, 'Show me every pitch Wainwright has ever thrown me.' We can filter it down. If they want to see only the curveballs, we can do that. If they want to see only the 1–0 pitches, we can do that. The software is so impressive. Most of players and coaches are really good at using it now. They catch on very quickly."

One of the biggest advances prompted by the video-analytics revolution has been in the area of defensive positioning. You see the elaborate and exaggerated shifts now that were not part of the game a generation ago. "The Brewers were, if not the first, one of the first to use radical shifts," Crawford said. "In 2004 we had Rich Dauer as a coach. He liked to be aggressive in shifts. He had a lot of paper spray charts. It took me and Karl a while to make him realize that we could give him where the ball was hit in every game, not just in the charts he kept from our games. He was using limited data. We told him, 'We know you're good at rowing the ship. But we've got better oars for you.' Once he bought into that, he ran with it. The ocean became his playground. We started doing some crazy shifts, and they started to take hits away. We would be on the road, and you'd hear the radio and TV guys on the video feed saying, 'What are these guys doing? I don't know why they're playing like this, blah, blah, blah,' and it was working. It was burning other teams, and they didn't like it, so they tried to tear it down. These days, everybody does it. It got to the point where there has been talk of banning the shifts because it's hurting offense in the game."

On a normal night, Crawford captures video of each pitch and charts the type of pitch, the location, and the result. He also plots where the runners moved and what the fielders did.

"I'm basically staring at a computer screen the entire game," he said. "And there are times in the game when players will come up and want to look at something and we'll help them. In the middle of a game, if someone wants to see an at-bat, they can look. Some guys look to see if they got hosed on a call. Others come up when they are slumping. Some guys are in every day. Others never come in at all. Everybody has a different way of doing things, but the one thing for sure is that the technology is part of the game."

If you consider the clubhouse like a business office, Crawford and the video people are a bit like IT support. They have to deal with frustrated co-workers. "That's baseball," he said. "We're together all day, almost every day. No other sport is like that. Everybody gets on each other's nerves sometimes or where you just don't feel like working that day. In my job it's about player and coach satisfaction. I've got to check myself if I'm being grumpy or if I feel like I'm being inconvenienced. It's my job. I also have to remember that things I feel are no-brainers— just click here and here—can be complicated for other people. I do techy things and assume everyone automatically can do things with computers. I had to teach myself how to use the stuff, so I have to remember that."

Players often enter the video room and ask Crawford for his opinion. *Was I safe or out? Was that a strike or a ball?* Those can be tough questions to answer in the heat of battle. "I learned early on not to give my honest opinion," he said, laughing. "I'll say, 'I didn't see it,' or 'It was close. I need to see it again.' Eventually, most guys will come back and say, 'He got me.'

"Some guys come up as soon as an at-bat is over, watch, and their opinion is not colored by their own feelings or emotion. One of the best was Prince Fielder. He was incredible that way. He would look at a pitch and say, 'That was a strike.' Carlos Lee was like that, too. It was amazing what he could pick up watching video. Those were two guys who knew how to use it the right way."

Some guys look to video to find an edge against opponents. Others use it to end slumps or extend hot streaks. Crawford is ready either way. "As long as I have the technology, I can get players the video they're looking for," he said. "I might not be able to get that pretty blonde in Section 200, but other than that…"

Instant Replay

The advent of instant replay has added another wrinkle to the video operation. Scott Campbell, assistant director of video scouting, and Brian Powalish, the manager of advance scouting, work on compiling hitting and pitching scouting reports and also help monitor close calls and relay information to the bench coach about whether or not the Brewers should challenge a call. "That is a tough job," Crawford said. "It's a job where 15 seconds can feel like two seconds. They pause the live action, and you try to find an angle from the television feed that lets you make a decision—one way or another. Usually, it's the slo-mo angle, and that's the last one they show. It's a tough job, but those guys do it well. It's an in-game element that can change a game."

Brewers coach Jerry Narron was charged with contacting Campbell and Powalish when plays were close. "It's always important to trust the information you're getting," Narron said. "Joe knows the strike zone and the pitches, and we trust the information he gets in there. It's the same thing with Scott and Brian. They've done it enough that we trust them completely. That's huge."

Crawford agreed. "Every out is important," he said. "But if a run is involved, they're not going to call down and say 'Challenge this' unless they know there is a good chance it's going to be overturned."

When a play is close, Campbell and Powalish spring into action. "They're checking every bang-bang play," Crawford said. "If anything is questionable, they know the phone is going to ring."

Though video replay has led to a decrease in on-field arguments, manager ejections and—most important—blatantly missed calls, the system isn't perfect. "We had a call go against us in Cleveland," Crawford said. "I think it was Shane Peterson, sliding into a base. It was a really close play, and we were deciding whether or not to challenge, and the super slo-mo replay didn't come in until really late. That was the only angle that showed that he was safe. We tried to pick up the phone, but it was too late. The next guy had already stepped into the box. We got screwed on that one."

Under the current setup, umpires rotate through headquarters in New Jersey and conduct video replays. "It'd be better if they had the same guys in there looking at video for all 162 games," Narron said. "I think it was [Chicago Cubs manager] Joe Maddon who said, 'A bunch of nerds in there would do a better job.' I definitely trust the umpires, but when you're in there every day, it's an advantage."

Crawford pointed out that replay isn't made to interpret baseball rules. "It's really straightforward," he said. "Was the ball there first, or did the foot hit the bag? You don't have to say, 'I played 15 years in the big leagues' in order to determine if the ball hit a chalk line. It either did or it didn't."

Narron would like to see replay expand to cover more types of calls rather than safe/out or fair/foul. "We're not going to ask for replays unless we know there is a good shot of something being overturned," he said.

Crawford would like to see more time allotted for reviews. "We need the slo-motion replay as soon as possible," he said. "People forget how many angles we're looking at when we're trying to make a call. In times like that, 15 seconds feels like forever. But, you want to be right."

Team Travel

It's the seventh inning of a Wednesday night road game in San Diego. The Brewers are wrapping up the second leg of a three-city West Coast trip. It's getaway night, which means Milwaukee's traveling party—players, coaches, medical staff, and broadcasters—will be getting on a plane roughly 90 minutes after the game and flying to San Francisco, where the team will enjoy its first day off in several weeks. In the middle of the seventh inning, the Brewers lead 10–1. The starting pitcher is cruising. The bullpen is rested. The San Diego Padres look a little...let's be diplomatic and say "disinterested" in the final three innings.

In the booth Brian Anderson and I are talking about how nice and relaxing this game seems for the manager, players, and staff. It seems like a perfectly timed mental break heading into the day off. It's a game when the manager can rest his closer and critical relievers, get some key players a few innings of rest, and generally put his feet up and enjoy a few low-stress innings. We know that many fans watching in Wisconsin feel the same way and are likely heading to bed because it's a school night. The broadcast takes on a bit of a relaxed tone. We can have fun, tell some stories, and talk about our plans for the day off in San Francisco.

Any day off during the season is a precious commodity. Days off at home are generally preferable to days off on the road because players can sleep in their own beds, spend time with their families, and run some overdue errands—haircuts, dry cleaning, dental appointments, etc. Given a choice most players would rather spend time in their home city. San Francisco is an exception. Most players love the shopping, sightseeing, weather, culture, golf, wine, and nightlife that the Bay Area offers, so this is an eagerly awaited spot on the calendar. Chicago, Miami, New York, and Phoenix are also exceptions, but it also depends on the player. Guys from the Midwest love visiting St. Louis or Kansas City if it means they can visit family. I love going to Philadelphia because I get to see plenty of relatives and friends and eat cheesesteaks.

Anything can happen in baseball, but a 10–1 lead in the seventh is about as comfortable as you can get during the long season. Even though we won't board the plane for a while, the landing gear is down, and *almost* everyone can relax. But the idea of a relaxing day on the road is a foreign concept for Dan Larrea, who is wrapping up his second decade as the Brewers' director of team travel. Larrea has to worry about the truck that will haul the equipment from Petco Park to the airport. He has to worry about the buses that will take players and coaches to the tarmac in San Diego and from the San Francisco airport to the hotel. He has to make sure the hotel is ready with room keys in the lobby and bell staff to deliver luggage to rooms. And he has to worry about the airplane and the curfew for taking off in San Diego.

If you think about the details involved in moving all the players and their equipment, the number of things that can potentially go wrong is mind-boggling. Being the director of team travel—a modern update on the title traveling secretary—is one of the most thankless jobs in sports. It's a little like being an umpire because the only time people notice you is when things go badly.

Larrea has been in the job since 1997. He began working in sports two years earlier as a media relations intern with the Denver Broncos. "That was Mike Shanahan's first year as coach and the year they drafted running back Terrell Davis," Larrea recalled. "I moved to Milwaukee to join the Brewers' media relations department, and two years later, [Denver] won the Super Bowl."

How does one go from being in the media relations department, working on game notes, press releases, and statistics to coordinating travel? "My predecessor [as Brewers traveling secretary], Steve Ethier, accepted a job in stadium operations, and I got a call in February saying the job was open," Larrea said. "I was encouraged to apply and flew to spring training, which had already started, to interview with Sal Bando, who was our general manager at the time. I had zero experience. The interview was really Sal telling me about the job. Two or three days later, I was offered the position. Spring training was already underway, so I went to Chandler, which is where we trained, and started getting in the flow of things. Steve was there for a week, helping me. After that I was left alone on an island."

A lot of team travel arrangements are made during the winter. Today, the club flies with a single air carrier (United) for charter flights. Back in the late 1990s, the team used more than a dozen different carriers and even flew on a few commercial flights. Travel, as Larrea quickly discovered, is just part of the job. "In my first year, I basically had an outline of what I needed to get accomplished for spring training: meal money, tickets, buses. Those are the three basic things in spring training. The regular season was a little different. I got through the first season okay and what did we do? We moved from the American League to the National League. So you go through your first year, you meet all the hotel reps, you handle all the bus companies, you deal with airports and officials in the road cities. Then we switched leagues, and I was basically learning the job all over again."

Although team travel directors get plenty of free advice, especially from players when planes are delayed or hotel accommodations have hiccups, there is no help desk they can turn to in an emergency. "You can bounce things off other people in the business, but there are 30 teams, and they have 30 different ways of doing things," Larrea said. "For example, everybody has a different interpretation of the collective bargaining agreement. Let's say a player gets called up from the minor leagues. Some teams will pay for that player's car to be shipped [from the minor league city to the major league city.] Players are allocated a certain amount of moving expenses, but nothing stipulates what those expenses are. Other than flying the player and his family to the big league city, it doesn't say, 'We'll pack up. We are responsible to handle a semi and shipping of your furniture.' It doesn't say, 'We will ship one car' or, 'We will ship two cars.' And what type of shipping are we talking about? Is it covered? Is it open-air? All these things are not minor, but they are questions that are asked by the player and by ourselves. They all cause differentiation of price. Some of these guys have very nice cars. They want to have a covered shipment, which I fully understand. Is that the club's obligation to make sure that his car isn't exposed to dirt and elements upon shipment? That's open to interpretation. Basically, MLB's thought process on this is that they leave it to teams' past practice. They don't give an answer and they say, 'What have you done before? Okay, do that.'"

Once teams settle into a pattern of travel—with an airline, bus companies, hotels—it can be hard to get them to change. "If changes come, it's often because of price," Larrea said. "We fly a 737-800 plane, and the price is based on a block-hour rate. Because we are in the Central Division, our charter prices are lower than clubs like Seattle, Miami, San Francisco, or San Diego. For a while a lot of teams were flying with Delta. Then they decided to change the type of aircraft for major league charters. For some teams the budget went up by $500,000 to $700,000. Many teams left and went with United, but that airline only wanted to accommodate a certain number of teams because too many would possibly cause a disruption of their regular service."

Like any business traveler, Larrea has to deal with mechanical issues, crew deadlines and other problems. "Most people don't realize that our planes don't show up until two hours prior to the departure time that I stipulate," he said. "That means it's showing up from another city. Well, if there are any weather disruptions across the U.S., we could possibly be impacted."

If the Brewers' travel is impacted by a few hours—say that a plane arrives in a city at 5:00 AM rather than 2:00 AM—it can make a difference on the field. Sleep is important for athletes, which is why hotels are important, and Larrea is careful to select the right one. "There are probably three or four criteria," he said. "It's got to be a first-class hotel, per the collective bargaining agreement. We want to stay in a nice hotel regardless, but that's first. The second criteria is the service provided by the hotel to the team. We have to make a large number of requests. We want to ensure that the hotel meets all those requests and does it in a way that benefits players. The third criteria is location. Proximity to the ballpark is important. The last thing we look at is if they've handled pro sports teams before. Certain hotels can have great service, but things will fall through the cracks if they don't know how to handle a pro sports team."

Although certain teams prefer different hotel chains, it is common for one or two hotels to handle all the big league business in a certain city. On the road the hotel becomes Larrea's office. He wakes up in the morning and starts handling phone calls and emails about travel arrangements and player requests. The first bus leaves the hotel five hours before game time, and the second bus leaves three hours before game time. Generally speaking, the second bus is for broadcasters and that night's starting pitcher, who is allowed to arrive a little later than his teammates.

When Larrea arrives at the ballpark, he begins working on players' complimentary tickets. All big league players and coaches submit their ticket requests into a computer system that tracks all the complimentary tickets used throughout the year on a per-game basis. They did that a few years ago that for taxation purposes. At most ballparks the visiting team receives between 220 and 250 tickets for players and traveling staff. Roughly half of those seats, though, are in the upper deck. Some teams like the Dodgers can make things difficult on Larrea by giving tickets in strange configurations (i.e. one in front, three behind). "I have to move things around a bit," Larrea said.

When the tickets are allocated, Larrea focuses on buses, luggage and equipment, and hotel arrangements. The Brewers have employed a new luggage tracking system that uses bar codes to keep track of everything. Some players have contracts that give them suites on the road, so he has to make sure those are ready and any other personal requests are handled.

"I generally send a three-page document to the hotel, and it goes through all my expectations for a trip," Larrea said. "If somebody's wife is coming in, she needs to be on the rooming list to receive a key so that somebody just can't portray herself as a wife and get a key. The hotel must contact me if there are any changes to a hotel reservation. They cannot do it without my confirmation."

Larrea said the toughest part of his job is anticipating problems that haven't occurred yet. More often than not, decisions are made in minutes. "One year, we were departing Detroit right before the All-Star break," he said "The plane was coming in from Rio de Janeiro and it was delayed. Luckily, it was right before the break, so about half the players were departing to their home or some other location. So I had to scramble. I got two 16-seat jets. We had 16 staff and 15 players. We did a players' plane and a staff plane and we trucked our equipment back from Detroit to Milwaukee. People liked it. They didn't really say anything. Most people had not been on a private plane like that before, so it was a unique experience. And it was only a 50-minute flight. But [setting that up] was very stressful."

JEFF CIRILLO'S NEAR TRAVEL DISASTER

In 1997 Brewers third baseman Jeff Cirillo was selected to the All-Star team for the first time in his career. He and his wife, Nancy, were heading to Cleveland for the festivities at Jacobs Field, when a fan recognized him aboard the plane, and the following exchange took place. "Are you Jeff Cirillo?" the fan asked.

"Yes, I am," Cirillo said.

"Are you going to the All-Star Game?" the fan asked.

"Yes, I am," Cirillo said.

"Then, what are you doing on a flight to Newark?" the fan asked.

"What do you mean?" Cirillo asked. "We're going to Cleveland."

Jeff Cirillo hits a game-winning home run in 1997, a year in which he was selected to—but almost missed—the All-Star Game.

"No, we're going to Newark."

The fog of morning, coupled with Cirillo's excitement about the trip, prompted him to miss a gate change. "They said it was Gate 24, so that's where we went," Cirillo said. "But they switched it to Gate 26, and I didn't know it. I gave the lady our tickets and I guess she didn't really look at them. We were on our way."

Cirillo, whose uniform number with the Brewers at the time was 26 (just like the gate), got off the plane before it departed and barely made it onto a flight for Cleveland just before the doors closed. He made it to town in time for the press conferences and workout that precede the Home Run Derby. "That would have been embarrassing," he said. When it was pointed out that Cirillo was lucky to be recognized, he deadpanned a line for the ages: "Yeah, I was traveling under my alias, Jeff Cirillo."

When you're always traveling with the team on the road and in hotel rooms, you're going to have some weird things happen from time to time. I remember my TV partner, Matt Vasgersian, had one memorable encounter. I forget what city we were in, but we had played a day game and flew to the next town and arrived at our hotel at about 9:00 in the evening. We got our key, and everybody headed up to their rooms to put their computer bags away and we were going to meet in the lobby and go out to grab a beer and watch a game on TV.

Vasgersian, who is a bit of a germophobe, put his key in the door, walked in, and got the shock of a lifetime. The bathroom door was open and there was a man sitting on the toilet. "He was reading the Life section of that day's USA TODAY," Vasgersian said. "I startled him, and he jumped up. I jumped, ran to the front desk, and demanded a new room."

You never know what is going to happen when you put your card key in the door.

One year, we were in Seattle. Everybody was out at a place called the Celebrity Club. I stumbled back to my room late at night and went to brush my teeth. I unzipped my shaving kit and I froze. I couldn't move. There was a little green turd in the middle of it. I froze. Somebody was messing with me. I zipped it back up and threw it in the trash. I figured I'd replace everything the next day. I went to the ballpark, suspecting it was the work of Rick Cerone, who was known for scatological pranks. I was really worked up. I was going to let Cerone have it and the first person I saw when I got to the ballpark was our coach, Frank Howard. Hondo was livid. He looked at me and said, "Billy, I smelled crap."

I said, "What?"

He repeated: "Billy, I smelled crap."

It turned out that Hondo had gone to bed that night, pulled back the sheets, and someone had dropped a deuce in the bed. He went downstairs and immediately changed rooms.

Apparently, Cerone was on a binge.

Not all hotel mishaps are that messy (or disgusting). Sometimes room service can be an adventure, too. A few years ago, we were in Los Angeles for a series at Dodger Stadium and we were staying at the Hyatt Regency Century Plaza in Century City. I like to drink coffee in the morning, and most of our hotels have coffee makers in the room. I got up in the morning, made a pot of coffee and I noticed that there wasn't any cream or sugar in the room. I like my coffee with cream and sugar, so I called to room service, explained my situation, and asked if they could send some condiments to my room.

A few minutes later, there was a really faint tap on the door. I opened it, and there was a very short woman with a baseball cap pulled way down over her head, which made it hard to see her eyes. She reached her hand out, I grabbed what was in her hand, thanked her, and closed the door. I walked a few steps toward the coffee pot, looked at my hand, and realized she had handed me two condoms. There was a note that said, "Enjoy your stay."

I couldn't believe it. I was wondering if anybody was messing with me. Who is going to send condoms to my room? I was scratching my head. I was wondering which member of the traveling party would do that. Then, it hit me. I had asked for *condiments*. The woman from room service—who didn't speak English very well—thought I said *condoms*.

I was embarrassed. I called back down because I didn't want her to think I was a freak. I calmly explained that I did not order condoms but had asked for condiments. I apologized for not specifying cream and sugar. The woman acted like she had just run over my dog. She was horrified. "Sir, please don't tell my boss," she said. "Don't call the desk. I'll take care of it." A few minutes later, they sent me a nice pot of coffee with some toast and a whole bunch of cream and sugar. That was a weird way to start the day, but it was nowhere near as weird as the way my day ended in Colorado in about 2010.

My son, Billy, had just joined the Army, was weeks away from going to boot camp, and came into Denver for a three-game series. We were hanging out after the game and we went to the Tilted Kilt restaurant to have a few beers and some chicken wings with some guys from the TV crew and a couple of the coaches, including third-base coach Ed Sedar and Dale Sveum, my buddy and former teammate, who was the hitting coach. We were hanging out, having a good time, and my son started to hit it off with one of the waitresses. Well, Billy and I were sharing a room during the series, and I figured he didn't need his old man hanging around so I decided to leave him there with Dale and Eddie.

A while later, I was sound asleep in my room and I got a sense that something wasn't quite right. I opened my eyes and I saw Dale. He was laying right in front of me, his face inches from mine with a stupid grin on his face and a dip in his mouth. He scared the hell out of me. My first instinct was to push him away. He went flying into the wall and I looked down and realized he was naked. I was in a panic. I started to sit up and I felt a tap on my shoulder and I heard Eddie, who has the most distinctive voice this side of Bob Uecker or Brian Anderson, say, "Hey, Rock! It's me and Dale. And we're *naked!*"

I turned around, and there was Eddie. I didn't know what was happening. I thought it was a bizarre dream but slowly started to figure out that Dale gave Billy the key to his room, and my son, in his infinite wisdom, had given Dale the key to our room. These two idiots decided to mess with me by hopping into the bed naked. As I sat there, rubbing my eyes and trying to get my heart rate to return to normal, Eddie and Dale started to get dressed in the little hallway by the bathroom. Suddenly, Dale stopped and said, "What am I getting dressed for? I'm not going anywhere." With that, he jumped into Billy's bed and within 15 seconds he was snoring. Eddie got dressed and yelled, "Bye, Rock. It was good seeing you...naked." It took me about an hour to get back to sleep. I was totally freaked out, but Eddie and Dale and I still laugh about "the Attack of the Naked Idiots." It's the greatest prank ever pulled on me. Needless to say, my son had a much better night than I did.

Batting Practice

Although it only happens once a day, batting practice is a bit like brushing your teeth. It occurs without much forethought or after-thought, but it's an indispensable part of a baseball player's daily ritual. It's a comforting call to order. It's hard to imagine life without it. It's also hard to explain.

According to research provided by the National Baseball Hall of Fame and Museum, batting practice dates to the mid-1880s. Back then, as noted by *A Game of Inches* author Peter Morris, "hitting was viewed as an instinctive skill that could not be learned or taught." In the days before mass production, owners were reluctant to waste or damage baseballs that could be used in games. Batting practice became more structured in the early 1900s and hasn't changed a great deal in half a century.

When fans watch players maneuver through different drills, work-ing behind protective screens, moving in and out of the batting cage with coaches hitting fungoes and as many as five or six baseballs in play, it can be a tad confusing. Former Brewers catcher Jason Kendall referred to batting practice as a "war zone." Others have called it "controlled chaos," a "beehive," or a "sporting symphony." There is so much going on dur-ing the session that it's hard for people to understand the activity. It can be confusing for outsiders. Imagine driving a stick shift in a car. When you're learning, coordination between the clutch and the stick shift can seem awkward and not at all intuitive. Once you've mastered it, though, it's second nature, and you don't give it a lot of thought. Batting practice is like that.

When players get traded, they may have trouble adjusting to new ballparks, teammates, coaches, front-office executives, security guards, clubhouse attendants, hotels, traffic patterns, and a myriad of other things. But they'll find comfort in the ritual of batting practice, which varies little from one team to the next and hasn't changed a great deal in generations.

In order to fully understand batting practice, one must realize that it is just a part—albeit a big part—of the pregame ritual. If the ballgame is slated to start at 7:10 PM, coaches and managers start showing up around 12:30 or 1:00 PM with players trickling in at various times after. Every player has a routine and a "comfort zone" when it comes to arriving for work, but the culture in baseball dictates that players arrive long before it's required.

On the first day of spring training, many managers will pass out a printed sheet of about seven or eight team rules. Invariably, Rule No. 1 is: "Be on time." At every level of professional baseball, "on time" generally means "early." Younger players and hard core veterans, like the aforementioned Kendall, often show up with the coaches. Rookies are usually expected to arrive for early work or because they are expected to get treatment or use the weight room earlier than veteran players. Established players have their own routines, but they generally arrive between 2:30 and 3:00 PM. The starting pitcher for a particular game is the last player to arrive because they don't take part in team stretching and pregame activity. They go out and warm up on their own schedule. Some relievers also arrive later because many times they have to do their conditioning work after the game in case they are required to pitch on a given night.

Now if you were to watch a live feed of clubhouse activity beginning when players arrive, what you see might not be described as "work" in the classic sense. You will see guys moving between the indoor batting cage, the training room, the weight room, and the video room. But you'll also see guys in their underwear, playing video games on their iPhones, watching movies on the sofa, playing cards, eating lunch, and planning pranks.

There is little question that players spend more time in the clubhouse than they do actually playing. Business efficiency experts might say that a lot of time in baseball is wasted, but every player knows what he needs to do in order to be ready for that night's game. Players and coaches can look at video, go over scouting reports, and work in the batting cage and weight room at his own pace and intensity level. Like many offices the conversations aren't always work-related. You'll hear guys talking about restaurants, hunting trips, wives, kids, girlfriends, agents, politics, religion, music, fantasy football, and just about everything else under the sun, but baseball is never far from the conversation.

Younger players will talk to and observe older guys in order to get a feel for what it takes to be in the big leagues. Early work is a catch-all phrase used to describe anything that happens outside of the team stretching and batting practice. It generally gets underway at about 2:00 PM and can include extra batting practice, soft toss, tee work, and bunting practice. It might include conditioning and pitcher's fielding practice (PFP). Catchers might work on blocking balls in the dirt. If Scooter Gennett is having trouble with his footwork on a double play, he'll be out there with a couple coaches working on it before the game. Outfielders may work on going back on balls near the fence. On the road early work can be crucial. Players need to be aware of the nuances of each park. Is the infield grass long and thick, or is it cut smooth like a putting green? Is the backstop under the screen behind home plate padded? Is it made of brick? Is there a rotating advertising billboard behind the plate? All of those things can impact the game.

At Miller Park the outfield warning track is a little wider than at many parks around baseball. You'll often see visiting players hesitate as they run near the wall. That can be the difference between a two-out, run-scoring triple and long out. Early work is a good time to get familiar with the surroundings and to brush up on fundamentals. When second baseman Rickie Weeks began his career with the Brewers, the coaches worked with him constantly on drills to improve his defensive footwork and throwing, and he made huge strides in that department. Early work is especially important for younger players and those who aren't receiving steady playing time. It's almost like their gameday. You see them come in after early work, and they are soaked with sweat. Though they have to be careful not to overextend themselves, the bullpen guys often have their own version of early work.

When Trevor Hoffman pitched for the Brewers, he brought an intense workout routine that many fellow relievers followed. "Camp Hoffman" included long runs around Miller Park, abdominal, and agility work, and even running pass patterns and throwing footballs for extra conditioning work. "Trevor is like 90 years old, and he's in better shape than everybody," reliever Seth McClung joked after completing one of the "Camp Hoffman" workouts, which continued under the watch of subsequent closers John Axford and Frankie Rodriguez.

Early work is generally the only time, outside of early spring training sessions, when you'll find players and coaches in shorts and T-shirts. It's an informal setting, but the work being done is often pretty serious. Most afternoons at home include a round of pitchers' batting practice, and that is a time when you'll hear a lot of hooting and hollering. Brewers bullpen coach Marcus Hanel throws batting practice to the pitchers, most of whom use enthusiasm and bravado to compensate for a lack of actual hitting prowess. Pitchers' BP is limited to starters and usually a long reliever because they are the guys who need it. There is a lot of work on bunting and some situational drills like the butcher boy play, when

When he was a closer with the San Diego Padres and Milwaukee Brewers, Trevor Hoffman was known for his intense pregame workouts.

hitters will square around to bunt and then chop a swing to try and catch the defense off guard or out of position. At the end of the round, pitchers usually have some kind of competition going. It can be a daily thing or something that carries through an entire season. On the rare occasion that someone hits a ball out of the park, you'll hear a half-dozen players screaming in the empty stadium.

At about 4:15 on most days, position players head out for a team stretching session. The tone of that is generally not very serious. If you watch from the dugout or the stands, it looks pretty relaxed. Strength coach Josh Seligman usually presides over the activity, but players are often talking and laughing and seem to be going through the motions. The thing to remember is that most of them have already been doing things in the weight room, batting cage, or on the field. The stretching routine is another thing that is part of the ritual.

In the 1980s and early '90s, then-Brewers trainer John Adam led the daily stretching session and kept up a running monologue that would give Jimmy Kimmel, Stephen Colbert, Johnny Carson, or any other late-night TV host from any era a run for his money. Known as "Quincy," Adam—who now works as a head athletic trainer and administrator for the PGA Tour—is regarded by most who encountered him as one of the funniest men in baseball. He would get on players about their eating habits, drinking habits, their slumps, their slumpbusters, and just about anything else that drifted into mind. There are some days when players have to drag themselves out of the clubhouse or off the bench to hit the field for team stretching. When "Quincy" was in charge, guys couldn't wait.

After team stretching is completed, the fun starts. Some guys will play catch. Pitchers go to the outfield to shag balls. And the activity on the field heats up. One of the first thing fans might notice during batting practice is the presence of screens, which are placed in front of the pitcher, in front of first base and both in front of and behind second base. These are positioned to protect the pitcher, obviously, along with players who take throws at first base, fielders in the middle infield, and the coach who hits fungoes to outfielders. Balls hit to the outfield are thrown toward the outfield screen, where they are collected in a bucket and returned to the mound to be used in batting practice. At one time baseball tradition held that the previous night's starting pitcher was on "bucket duty." Over time, though, players began tipping bat boys (or other players) to do it for them. Today, that duty falls to a team attendant or coach.

Brewers third-base coach Ed Sedar is in charge of organizing the pregame workout, which means he gets to set the hitting groups. Generally speaking, hitters are divided into four groups of three or four players, and they get 12 to 15 minutes in the cage. For most teams the groups are loosely aligned with the batting order. The first three batters form Group 1, the next three are Group 2, the bottom three (excluding the pitcher in the National League) are in Group 3, and Group 4 is the reserve players. The Brewers often group players by position. The three starting outfielders will hit in Group 1, where they are often joined by starting catcher Jonathan Lucroy, who gets his hitting in and then heads inside to go over the scouting report with the starting pitcher and pitching coach.

Each hitting group has a designated leader, who hits first and keeps track of the time and the number of swings in each round. Fans might think that hitters just grip it and rip it during batting practice like high-handicap golfers do on the driving range. There, however, is a little more structure to it than that. Just as pro golfers start with a wedge and work their way up to the driver, baseball players warm up slowly. The first three rounds of batting practice are pretty standard. At the start of each group, the first player steps into the cage and drops down two bunts—one toward first base and the other toward third. He then takes two swings, trying to hit the ball to the opposite field and three swings, trying to hit up the middle.

After his last swing of the round, the first batter will run to first base to work on base-running fundamentals like "cutting" the bases, which is baseball-speak for turning left as efficiently as possible. As the next batter begins hitting, the first hitter will work on getting a secondary lead and will run from first to second, second to third and third to home, working on secondary leads, reading balls off the bat, and timing his trip around the bases with pitches to the hitter.

If you want to see if a player is concentrating during batting practice, watch him stand at third base when it's his turn to run. If the batter hits a fly ball, he should go back and tag up. If it's a line drive, he should freeze. If the ball is hit on the ground, he should treat it like a "contact" play and break for home. If you see the guy just cruise down the line, you can guess that he's probably thinking about his swing and not really focusing on running fundamentals.

During the second round of BP, the focus is on situational hitting. The first swing is a hit-and-run approach. Right-handed batters try to shoot the ball toward second base. Lefties aim for the hole at shortstop. The second swing is a get-'em-over approach, where the hitter assumes there is a man on second and tries to hit the ball to the right side and advance the runner to third. On the third pitch, the hitter imagines a runner on third and the infield playing back. A ground ball will score the runner from third. The fourth pitch is a simulation of a man on third and infield in, so a fly ball to the outfield or a line drive or hard grounder up the middle are in order. The fifth pitch is a suicide squeeze bunt, where the batter has to put the ball in play. With those five things complete, the hitter gets two or three swings to hit away and then exits the cage. During this time hitting coach Darnell Coles watches and will review the scouting report of the opponent.

For the remaining four or five rounds, hitters are free to work on what they want. They usually start with five swings with the number diminishing each round until players are in the cage for just two pitches. The final rounds often feature longball fireworks. By this time hitters are loose and getting locked in. I remember watching Oakland A's sluggers Mark McGwire and Jose Canseco, at the peak of their days as the "Bash Brothers," hitting balls over the left-field wall at County Stadium. It was an incredible sight. During the "Great Home Run Chase" of 1998, McGwire, then playing for the St. Louis Cardinals, would take batting practice at Busch Stadium while the opposing team was stretching along the third-base line. Some players would pretend not to watch. Others would stare with their jaws agape and practically fall over laughing as McGwire treated Rawlings baseballs like Titleist golf balls.

Although every hitter approaches batting practice differently, most will agree that a good batting practice session does not necessarily lead to good at-bats in a game. The opposite is also true. There has been much debate about whether hitting a 65-mph pitch from a coach standing on a wooden ramp provides any meaningful preparation for hitters about to face 98 mph heat from someone like Detroit Tigers pitcher Justin Verlander. But batting practice is such a ritual that players often feel lost when they don't have it (like in day games or when rain or other events—like special pregame ceremonies—force postponement).

While fans focus on the hitters and the symphony of activity on the field, the batting practice pitcher behind the L-shaped screen often goes unnoticed. He's actually one of the more important guys on the field. Each coach usually throws to one group per day, which means he can throw about 120 pitches in 15 minutes. I'm always amazed that guys like Marcus Hanel, the Brewers' bullpen coach, throw early BP, pitchers' BP, and a regular group and seldom have arm trouble. By the end of the season, they are practically bionic.

Coaches often throw to the same group of hitters every day, so they can get used to tendencies. Hitters like pitches in a certain spot so they can work on things. Coaches become machine-like in their accuracy, but everybody can have a bad day once in awhile. Sometimes, hitters can get frustrated when they aren't getting pitches where they can drive them.

Billy Castro, the former Brewers pitcher and longtime bullpen coach, used to throw a heavy sinker and it wasn't uncommon for him to break a few bats in BP. Hitters weren't thrilled with that event, but it probably helped get them ready.

Most coaches throw from about a foot or two in front of the mound or about 50 feet from home plate. Ed Sedar, who has a natural motion and throws hard, would set up farther back. Dale Sveum would be very close, about 40 feet. His delivery would be a slower pitch, but the bottom line is that the swing speed and reaction time are very similar. Some teams—particularly those with older, injured, or non-throwing coaches—employ batting practice pitchers. If none of the coaches throws left-handed, it's common for teams to employ a left-handed BP pitcher in order to get hitters ready. Former Brewers manager Ron Roenicke is left-handed and he enjoyed throwing batting practice when the team was facing a lefty because it helped him gauge the adjustments hitters were making. Are they moving up in the box? Have they changed their hand position? Are they closer to the plate in order to hit pitches on the outer half? The problem for Roenicke—and most managers—is that batting practice is a time for interviews, radio shows, and other duties. That limits their availability to throw, but many will grab a fungo bat and hit grounders. Hitting grounders in batting practice also is a specialized duty that looks easier than it really is. Coaches wait until a split-second after the hitter in the cage makes contact, allowing fielders a chance to protect themselves from balls that can exit the bat at 110 mph.

Some coaches are adept at making ground balls spin, take tough hops, or hit spots that make players stretch to reach. You'll often see middle infielders work on double-plays during batting practice. That can be another "focus test." Is the player working to be balanced and deliver a good feed? Or is he flipping it behind his back? Sometimes, you'll see guys using their gloves to flip balls, but those situations can come up in games so it's not a bad idea to practice them. You'll see *SportsCenter* highlights of guys making behind-the-back feeds or glove flips in order to get outs.

While batting practice continues, Jonathan Lucroy and the pitching coach will be with the starting pitcher, going over the scouting report in a conference room across from the coaches' locker room. It's kind of an unwritten rule in baseball that you don't talk to the starting pitcher before a game. Some guys—like Kyle Lohse, Chris Capuano, and Yovani Gallardo—were the same, affable, approachable guys on pitching days and non-pitching days. Other pitchers go into the zone, and you are best to leave them alone. The scouting meeting, though, is when pitchers have to talk to Lucroy and the pitching coach. That meeting is when they will go over each hitter in the opposing lineup and talk about the best way to attack that hitter, using the pitcher's strengths to exploit a hitter's weaknesses.

If a batter likes the ball inside, you work him away and get him with soft stuff. If a guy shoots the ball to left field, pound him in. Some guys are more susceptible to the slider down and in, as opposed to the curveball. Lucroy is invaluable for these meetings because he knows the pitchers and the hitters. He'll also remember, *We got this guy out on a 2–0 change-up last time, so he'll probably be looking for a fastball in that count. Unless he tries to out-guess us and look for another change-up.*

Those discussions are important, but the scouting report is fluid once the game starts. You have to rely on what the pitcher has that night. Just like hitters, pitchers often have dazzling stuff in the bullpen and struggle in the game or vice versa. Hitters have their own scouting meetings, but that usually takes place on the first day of a series. They'll go over what the pitchers throw, what they like to do when they're ahead in the count or behind in the count. Does he throw a lot of first-pitch breaking balls? The information available to today's hitters is incredible. Many times, you'll see the opposing pitcher's last outing playing on TVs throughout the clubhouse before a game.

Sometimes, I wonder if guys suffer from information overload. Great hitters like Paul Molitor and Ryan Braun tend to remember how pitchers have worked them in the past. Every hitter takes mental notes, and some even keep a notebook for reference. But if you're at the plate with a man on third, and the count is 2–1, and you find yourself thinking *What did we say about 2–1 counts in the meeting this afternoon?*" I think you're already in bad shape.

After the first group—Brewers outfielders—finish their turn in the cage, the second group—the infielders—will head in. The guys who had previously been taking ground balls and working on relay feeds and throws to first base (where a coach usually catches them) get to hit while the out-fielders work on tracking balls off the bat or playing balls off the wall.

Throughout batting practice, you'll see pockets of pitchers stand-ing in the outfield shagging. Sometimes, you'll see guys run after balls in the gap and try to get a workout in. Other guys—especially those who have pitched a lot in recent games— keep the activity level low. The Brewers had a pitcher in the early '90s named Bill Wegman who used to fly around the outfield like a crazy person, trying to catch everything he could. In the final game of his final season with the club, Wegman convinced manager Phil Garner to let him play right field for an inning. Everybody on the team was on the top step of the dugout, hooting and hollering, but Weggy didn't get a ball hit his way.

Once you understand what is going on during BP, you see how scripted it is. It is like a dance sequence. Every once in a while, players or coaches will get hit by a baseball. When you consider how much is going on at one time, it's almost amazing that it doesn't happen more often. Midway through the 2015 season, Bob Uecker was standing behind the batting cage when someone hit a line drive off the L-screen in front of the pitcher. The ball caromed into the air and hit Uecker between the eyes before he knew what happened. He ended up missing the broadcast that night and spending the night in the hospital with concussion-like symptoms. "I'm always a little dizzy, but that was more than usual," Uecker joked.

Thankfully, Uecker recovered quickly. His injury, though, reminded me of a time years ago when a coach named Andy Etchebarren was hit during BP. "Etch" was a former catcher and he'd had a number of shoulder surgeries that made it impossible for him to lift his arm up over his head. So he'd throw batting practice with this God-awful arm angle. He'd throw this sidearm sinker that would barely get over the L-screen in front of the mound. In fact, every three or four days, he'd throw a pitch that would hit the screen and bounce back toward second base. Everybody laughed when that happened.

Nobody was laughing, though, when Jeffrey Leonard hit a line drive that smacked Etch between the eyes. He wobbled and fell down like a piano fell on him. Everybody was concerned. A few guys helped him into the training room, but the first thing he did was ask for a cigarette. Adam, who was the trainer, looked at Etch and asked, "Where did it hit you?" Etch said, "What do you mean where did it hit me?" And Johnny said, "I see 10 welts on your head. Which one was from the ball?"

When batting practice ends, some players will hang out on the field to say hello to friends from the other team. Others will sign autographs for fans. Others run to the clubhouse quickly in order to eat, shower, lift, stretch, or do whatever else gets them ready for the game. One of baseball's more confusing traditions, at least in my eyes, is that the home team has batting practice first. That means that when the gates open, fans usually see the opposing team take batting practice. That has never made sense to me. I know players like the extra rest, but they would get that on the road, where many of them arrive at the ballpark early out of sheer boredom. I think home fans want to see home players work out. It'd be an easy switch, but it'll probably never happen because batting practice hasn't changed a lot over the past 100 years.

PART V:
IN THE BOOTH

My Baseball Life

My parents were really the foundation of my baseball upbringing. My dad would take us to help with his team's practice and in his free time he would take us to an old sandlot and throw us batting practice and hit us ground balls. We would hit balls until the covers came off, tape them up with black electrical tape, and keep hitting them until they were practically oblong. There were no aluminum bats back then. Our bats would get worn out, and we'd put nails in them and keep hitting. My dad kept throwing and throwing, and this went on until the early days of high school. We didn't have any pitching screens or anything. And one day I hit one up the middle. I thought it was going to hit him right between the eyes. It missed him, and the ball was in the outfield by the time he ducked. At that point I think we all agreed that dad was done throwing me batting practice.

My father taught me a lot of fundamental things about the game. He was a teacher, so he made sure it came across in a positive way and that I understood why he was telling me to do things. I was becoming a pretty good player, but he made sure I didn't get a big head. I remember he would hit us ground balls for hours. He would stand near the mound, and we would stand in front of the backstop, which was smart because we didn't have to go chasing our misses. He would hit them from side to side, making my brother, Ed, work to cover ground. He would hit high hoppers and worm-burners and everything in between. When I missed one, he'd hit the next one a little bit harder. If I missed another, the next one would be harder still.

I learned how to concentrate in those practice sessions, and that never left me. In some ways those practices were tougher than the games. But I loved it. I loved baseball so much that he used to mess with me at times. When I was seven, eight, or nine years old, I would get so excited for games that I'd get really nervous if it looked like it was going to rain. My dad knew that and he would torment me. He would turn on the windshield wipers even if it wasn't raining. (This, of course, was back in the days before you could just look at your phone and see the radar.) I'd be so worried that the games were going to be canceled. I'd get so upset, and my dad would just laugh. We still joke about it. He is north of 80 years old now, and we still laugh about it.

He was really the foundation of my baseball career. He taught me the game at a young age and was a support mechanism all the way through college and the big leagues. He always pushed me to be better. Whether it was Little League or high school, I could go 4-for-5 with two home runs and a bunch of RBIs, and the only thing we'd talk about on the way home was my pop-up to center field in my third at-bat. He wanted to know what was going on in my head during that at-bat. He never let things get away from me, so I never really got full of myelf.

My mom was very supportive, too. She'd be at every game right there with my dad. If I had two games in a day, whether it was a school game followed by a Babe Ruth League or American Legion game, she was there watching and she'd have a full-blown meal for me in one of those cardboard beer boxes. She didn't feed me fast food or any of that nonsense. She would have pork chops, green beans, and mashed potatoes. I would sit in the backseat of the car and eat a full meal, change my uniform, and go to the next game. My parents were terrific. I can't even guess how many vacations they gave up because I was in All-Star Games or things like that.

My brother was always there with me, too. He was on a lot of teams that I was on. He actually saved a no-hitter for me in a Little League game. I was pitching, and we had two outs in the sixth inning. (We played six innings in those days.) A guy hit a rocket to right field, where my brother was playing, and he came in and made a shoestring catch and saved the no-hitter. That was a big day in the Schroeder household.

My family was there for me all the way through my career. For a lot of parents, their kids' youth or high school sports becomes their social hub. They hang out with other parents and gossip and have barbecues and they have carpools and travel to games together.

One thing I discovered early on is that my father didn't like to sit around and watch the game with all the other parents. He would go down the lines and watch by himself and concentrate on what was going on. The joke in our family was that when I made an out, he'd move to a new location. If I got a hit, he'd stay where he was. We laughed about that a lot because I said that he probably sat in every seat in County Stadium because I made a lot of outs in the big leagues. That always brings a laugh in our family. I made it to the big leagues and I played for eight years. I know that's a special accomplishment, but I wasn't a special player. I didn't have an outstanding career. I used to tell people, "I made all my outs in the big leagues. Where did you make yours?"

By the time I got to high school, it was clear that baseball was my best sport. I remember the high school wrestling coach wanted me to go out for his team, but there was no way I would do that. The idea of putting on tights and rolling around on a sweaty mat with another sweaty guy didn't appeal to me at all. I knew that the wrestlers were tough. I knew they were in great shape. I just didn't want any part of it.

I played basketball during the winter instead, and that was fun, but it was really just a way for me to stay in shape during baseball season. In New Jersey at that time, the high school baseball season was pretty short. We played about 25 games—provided they didn't get rained out or canceled because of cold weather. I remember playing games in high school when they'd have a big oil drum with a fire in it to help us keep warm. We didn't have aluminum bats back then. We used wooden bats, and it was so cold that I remember hitting with regular winter gloves. We, though, made the best of the situation. We played teams from around the area and did pretty well.

By the time I got to be a senior, I started to apply to colleges. I applied on my own to Rutgers, Georgia, and Clemson. I remember being crushed when I got turned down at Rutgers. My grades were average at best, but they didn't have to be great back in those days. I got turned down for early acceptance, and the baseball program wasn't interested in me either. The coach there was a guy named Ray Bolger. He didn't have the job very long. I don't know if it was a coincidence because he didn't want me there or what, but a couple years after I moved on to college, he was let go.

I got accepted at Georgia and Clemson. I applied to Vanderbilt, so I had some options. I wrote a letter to a congressman to explore going to one of the service academies—either the Naval Academy in Annapolis or West Point, but that didn't pan out. I wasn't smart enough. My baseball coach at West Windsor was Rex Walker. He knew that I wanted to go to Clemson. He made a phone call to Bill Wilhelm, who was the legendary coach there. Coach Wilhelm didn't take the call. Rex wrote a letter to Wilhelm, who wrote back that he wasn't interested. At this point Rex got a little upset. He called Wilhelm and left him a number of messages. He told him, "I have a kid here who is a catcher, and he can throw and he can hit and I can't believe that you won't even take a look at him."

Finally, Wilhelm told him he'd stop by for a game. He was college baseball royalty. Wilhelm had an unbelievable career at Clemson and did a lot of recruiting in New York, New Jersey, Virginia but not a lot in South Carolina, believe it or not. He went out of the box and he was very successful. He was on a recruiting trip, looking at other players in the area and he stopped by one of my games. My father was there, and Coach Wilhelm introduced himself.

Right away, I kind of got a little nervous. He was there to see if I could cut the mustard. I knew it was my big chance. I didn't usually get nervous before games, but this time was different. I thought it was do or die. And I played…like death.

I think I struck out three times, got an infield hit, and threw a ball into center field on a stolen base attempt. I was feeling horrible, and after the game, Coach Wilhelm offered me a scholarship. I'll never forget it.

He said he wasn't worried about the results; he was looking at the fundamentals. He was looking at my footwork behind the plate and how I set up to catch the ball. He was looking at my batting stance and my offensive approach. Apparently, he had talked to a number of scouts before he came to see me, and they all told me that I'd be a good fit at Clemson.

It was a dream come true for me. A couple months later, my father, mother, and brother packed up and drove down to Clemson. My dorm room, which was for baseball players, was a fraternity house. We had an entire floor of a fraternity house! I got there, and my roommate wasn't there yet. I was in there for two days alone, just walking around campus and checking things out. Finally, my roommate, Gene Wisniewski, showed up. It was a match made in heaven. He was from Philadelphia; I was from New Jersey. We hit it off right away and got along tremendously.

I didn't play a lot. Bill Foley was there. He was a catcher from New York who got drafted by the Brewers. I played some left field, I was the designated hitter, I caught. I remember hitting my first collegiate home run at The Citadel. It went out to right field. To this day I remember circling the bases and I don't think my feet touched the ground. We did pretty well in the ACC that year and we ended up going to the College World Series. Paul Molitor was there, playing shortstop for Minnesota. I caught one game in that World Series, going 2-for-5 at Rosenblatt Stadium against Temple University. It was the only game that we won there.

The next two years were a lot of fun. I loved going to Clemson, being on the team, and playing for Wilhelm. He was a lot like my father because he worked me hard. I remember one game we played in Virginia. It was my sophomore or junior year. I was pretty awful that day. I struck out three or four times. Now, back then we didn't have a big coach bus to go to games. When we played schools that were close by, like Duke, Maryland, or Virginia, we took a bunch of vans. They were six or eight-passenger vans. We'd take three or four of them to the games, a lot of which were played on Saturday afternoons.

Well, the coaches would give the keys to somebody, so we could go out with whatever meal money we had and get something to eat. I was standing in the back of the group, feeling dejected because I'd had a bad game with a couple of punch-outs and we had lost, and somebody asked Wilhelm, "Who do you want to have the keys?" His response was, "Give them to Schroeder. At least I know he's not going to hit anything with it."

Everybody cracked up. I laughed, too. The tension was broken, and I think I got three hits the next game. Wilhelm was a tough customer. He always wanted me to do better. At times, I think he and my father were working together to keep me humble. They both used the same techniques on me and I needed it.

I really enjoyed Coach Wilhelm. In 36 years at Clemson, he had a won-lost record of 1,161–536 –10. That's amazing. He was inducted into the National College Baseball Hall of Fame in 2011. He's also in the South Carolina Athletic Hall of Fame and the Clemson Athletic Hall of Fame. And the stadium is named after him. I was able to reconnect with him before he died and I'm glad I did. He meant a lot to me.

* * *

After my junior year at Clemson wrapped up in the spring of 1979, I was drafted by the Milwaukee Brewers. Although I'd heard of the Brewers, I didn't know anything about Wisconsin or Milwaukee—the state and city where I would end up spending most of my life. Toward the end of my junior year, I was selected to play for Team USA in the Pan Am Games. Jack Stallings, who was a legendary coach at Georgia Southern, held tryouts. I made that Pan Am team, so I was preparing at home to go meet with them in Miami. We were going to practice and go to Columbia to play the Pan Am Games.

When draft day came, I was sitting around the house, and we were barbecuing something on the grill. The Brewers called. For the life of

I swing the bat during my playing days with Brewers, which lasted six years. *(Courtesy: Milwaukee Brewers)*

me, I can't remember who it was. But I know Joe McIlvaine came to the house to present me with my contract, so it might have been him. Anyway, the call came that day. I was drafted in the eighth round, and the Brewers wanted me to show up for rookie ball in Butte, Montana, and begin my pro career.

I wasn't sure how any of this worked at the time, but we had an ace in the hole. One of the guys who was teaching with my father was named Rich Giallella. He had played at Rider College in the late 1960s and ended up having a six-year career in the minor leagues.

Rich was coaching me a little bit, telling me what questions to ask the Brewers. I was 20 years old. I didn't really know what was going on. Rich told me to ask the Brewers why they picked me in the eighth round, where would they send me, would I be able to play every day, etc. Some of the stuff was obvious. They weren't going to bring up money. He told me to mention that I had a year left in college and had opportunities to play in the Pan Am Games and in the Alaska Summer League.

Eventually, after about a week of back and forth, we came up with a figure of $15,000 for a signing bonus. I don't know how we got there. The Brewers seemed to think that was pretty high. Well, I was pretty excited about going to the Pan Am Games, and the idea of going back to Clemson for my senior year didn't seem too bad, so I told them I wasn't very interested. On a Sunday morning, I was sitting in my tan leisure suit, looking fine. Mom and Dad were sitting there, and we were getting ready to go to the airport in Philadelphia, so I could catch the Pan Am team in Miami.

Just as we were getting ready to leave—about 15 minutes before in fact—the phone rang. The Brewers offered me $15,000 for a signing bonus. For an eighth-round pick in 1979, that wasn't bad money at all. They wanted me to go to Butte. I immediately said, "Yes, I'll take it." But I wanted to call Jack Stallings to make sure he knew that I wouldn't be catching for him in Columbia. Whoever was on the other end of the phone said, "We've taken care of that. Don't worry. We told them you weren't coming. You're going to be a Milwaukee Brewer." That was the first time I realized that I was playing with the big boys now. They had already made the decision for me.

When I got to Montana, it was the culture shock of my life. First of all being a kid from New Jersey who played college ball in South Carolina, I didn't have much experience with the rugged, mountain terrain around Butte. I kind of felt like I was on the moon. John Hansen, who was a third-round pick from Hawaii, was my roommate. He gave me attitude the whole time I was there. I was an eighth-rounder. He felt like he was the big gun. Other than that, Butte was good to me. We had an apartment with four other guys, and it was within walking distance to the ballpark, which was actually the football stadium at Montana Tech. We dressed in the locker room in the gym and walked a quarter of a mile down a hill on a sidewalk to get to the stadium. I don't even know if there was a bathroom down there. I remember breaking off a cleat on my baseball shoes walking down the sidewalk. I played half the season with broken spikes.

The facilities weren't great, and the bus rides in the Pioneer League were long, but we didn't care. We were having the time of our lives. I was bringing home $192 every two weeks. My share of the apartment, which had no windows, was $35 a month. We never bought any food. We went to the M&M Cafe every night after the games for dinner. This place was half-bar, half-lunch counter. It opened in 1890 and was probably the model for every joint you've ever seen Guy Fieri visit on *Diners, Drive-Ins and Dives* on cable TV.

The M&M had a steak that was about a quarter-inch thick, french fries, and all the trimmings for $3.99. There was a woman we called "Mom" that waited on us. She had red, white, and blue curly hair. There was sawdust on the floor. Spitoons were everywhere. Dogs were running around. There was always a Keno game going on in the back. You could hear the numbers being called as we were sitting there. It was the time of my life.

Things were great on the field, too. In 65 games I hit .355 with 18 homers and 77 RBIs. I had 16 doubles, seven triples, and stole 18 bases. I played first base, caught and—lo and behold—made Hansen realize that he wasn't the big dog on campus. That would be me. In my second pro season, I went to Stockton in the Class A California League. I hit .268 with 18 homers (in almost twice as many at-bats) and drove in 97 runs. Looking at the stat line now, I cringe at the fact that I struck out 141 times in 437 at-bats. That was a sign of things to come, I guess. I remember playing on that team with guys like Jaime Cocanower, Doug Jones, Bob Gibson, Dion James, Eddie Irvine, and Bob Skube.

Our manager that year was Tony Muser, one of the great guys in baseball. We ended up going 90–51 and winning the California League championship that year, beating Visalia, which was managed by Tom Kelly. The next year didn't go as well. Playing for Double A El Paso, again under Muser, who was promoted with us, I had a bit of a down season. In 95 games in a hitter-friendly league, I ended up hitting .260 with 15 homers and 61 RBIs. I was wondering what kind of career I was going to have.

But the next two seasons at Triple A Vancouver perked me up again. I hit 22 homers and knocked in 77 runs in 1982. Our manager that year was Dick Phillips. In 1983 he let a promising lefty named Frank DiPino throw 189 pitches in a game. He was dismissed about two days later. Sam Suplizio took over on an interim basis, and then Muser got the job. It was Suplizio, a longtime roving instructor for the Brewers and friend to everyone, who gave me a call in mid-July telling me that Ted Simmons, Ned Yost, and Charlie Moore were all injured and that they needed me in Milwaukee.

I was on my way to the big leagues.

When I got the call, the Brewers were playing the Texas Rangers. I had to go to Arlington, Texas, for my first big league game. My teammate, Randy Ready, drove me to the Seattle airport, and my flight was delayed. I was supposed to be in the starting lineup that day, but I didn't get to the ballpark until about 20 minutes before the game so I was scratched. Harvey Kuenn, the manager at the time, put me in the next day, and my third time up I hit a triple, the only time I'd ever hit one in the big leagues.

The funny part of that was it wasn't supposed to be a triple. I was so excited to hit a ball over Billy Sample's head that I ran through a stop sign from Davey Garcia, the third-base coach. He had his hands up, and I never stopped running around second. The ball ended up hitting me in the back. It was my first—and only—triple in the big leagues.

I spent parts of the next eight years in the big leagues and loved every minute. I had two arm surgeries. I did six years with the Brewers and then went to the California Angels for two years. I made lifelong friends with whom I share some incredible memories.

Becoming a Broadcaster

When I finished playing, I didn't really know what to do with myself. I went back to Wisconsin. I actually never left Wisconsin. I was told one time by a very smart man, Paul Schramka, who owns Schramka Funeral Homes, that if you stick around Milwaukee and you're good to the people, the town will take care of you.

Well, it certainly has.

I've been very fortunate to have been a Wisconsinite and have lived here since 1984, when I first rented an apartment in the offseason. It's been very good to me. I owe a lot to the Seligs—Bud, Wendy, and Laurel Prieb—for giving me an opportunity.

When I got out of baseball, the first thing I did was enroll in Carroll College (now Carroll University) to finish the degree I started at Clemson. Fortunately, all of my credits transferred. I had one year left and went back full time. I think I needed 24 or 26 credits. I commuted back and forth from Hales Corners to Waukesha and got my degree. I was giving a speech to a Little League group in Cedarburg one evening and at the end I worked on the last piece of my graduation puzzle. I needed an internship. One of the requirements for graduation was having an internship. All the internships that Carroll offered seemed to be in Chicago. The last thing I wanted to do was drive to Chicago every day. So at the end of my speech, I kind of threw it out there. I told the crowd I needed an internship to finish my degree, and if anybody out there could help, I'd appreciate it.

Then the branch manager of the Paine Webber investment company came up to me. His name was Jim Carlson. He gave me his card and said, "Give me a call and I can help you out." Jim and I are still friends.

I got the internship. I finished it, got my degree, and passed the Series 7 exam. Paine Webber hired me, thinking that I had all these contacts. Well, I didn't really have that many. It was kind of a tough situation. I knew a few people, but they looked at me as an ex-baseball player or just a buddy to go out and have a drink with. They didn't really look at me as someone they wanted to manage their money. I guess I can understand that.

I had been doing a weekly Sunday baseball show on the Brewers' flagship radio station, WTMJ. I did it with a Milwaukee guy named Chuck Garbedian and Len Kasper, who is now the TV play-by-play man for the Chicago Cubs. After canceling the World Series in 1994, the baseball owners were intent on letting this be a "war to end all wars." They brought in replacement players the following spring and were threatening to start the season with them. Thankfully, it never got to that point. I actually got a call in February that year, when I was doing that weekly wrap-up show, an opportunity I got because of Brewers vice president of broadcast operations Bill Haig and I did it for two years. I enjoyed doing that and keeping abreast of what was going on with the club, though I never really hung out at the ballpark.

That was in that period of time where I had decided that I wasn't going to be hanging around the ballpark after my playing days. After two years with the Angels, I got my pink slip in October of 1990. For two years I never even attended a game. I didn't want to be one of those guys who hung around the clubhouse and was at the field with the players. It made it look like you had nothing better to do. Part of it was that I wasn't able to leave the game on my own terms like some players do. There are not many who do leave on their own terms. I certainly didn't.

Anyway, after staying away from the game for a bit, I was doing that call-in show for about two years. I got a call from Haig, saying I was in the running for the color analyst's job. I had lunch with Wendy Selig-Prieb at Balistreri's Bluemound Inn, which is near the ballpark, and she asked what I wanted to do. She wanted to know if my family was okay with me traveling on the road again. I said yes. Paine Webber was difficult for me. I was spending time cold-calling clients but not enough time. I knew that wasn't going to be a long-term solution for me and I also knew that I needed to work.

When you make it to the big leagues, people think you're automatically set for life in terms of your finances. For some guys, that may be true. If you sign a $50 million contract like Matt Garza or a $105 million extension like Ryan Braun, you can be pretty sure that your grandchildren will be taken care of financially. I wasn't in that class because of the era in which I played and my skill level. As a part-time player, I didn't make a lot of money. I was what we used to call a "point player." There were some guys making $1.2 million or $2.4 million. I was making the number after the decimal point. My largest salary as a player was $420,000. I made that my last two seasons, and they were my most injury-riddled years.

So I knew I needed a job, and getting back into baseball appealed to me on many levels. I remember I was on my way to watch a Milwaukee Admirals hockey game with my kids during a cold night in February. I love hockey, and the Admirals, who play in the American Hockey League, do a great job providing a fun night out in Milwaukee. As we were getting ready to go to the game, a call came at about 5:30 or 6:00 PM. Timing is everything in life. We didn't have cell phones in those days. I was just about to leave the house when the Brewers called. It reminded me of the call I got when I was getting ready to leave for Miami and the Pan Am Games, when Milwaukee offered me a pro contract and I accepted. This time Haig called and offered me the TV job. The schedule would only be 45 games, so I didn't make a lot of money. I don't even remember how much it was, but I knew that I didn't want to be a stockbroker anymore and I knew I was going to like working with Jim Paschke.

Paschke was a true pro, having worked as a local sportscaster and a play-by-play guy in baseball and basketball. It was his second go-around with the Brewers. He had initially worked as a play-by-play guy on television for Wisconsin Sports Network and in the early days of Midwest Sports Channel with Pete Vuckovich. Jim was a perfect first partner for me because I didn't know what I was doing. I got the job in 1995. The players were on strike, and the owners locked them out of spring training.

After accepting, I had lunch with Paschke and the producer/director of the broadcasts, Gary Kirby. We went to a Ground Round restaurant and had some chicken wings, and they started talking about camera placement and Chyron machines and audio and other technical things, and I had no idea what they were talking about. I started to worry that I was getting in way over my head. Finally, I asked, "Is there anything I can read?" I was looking for a book like *Baseball on TV for Dummies*, but such a thing didn't exist. I remember at the end of the lunch, Gary saw that I was uncomfortable and said, "Don't worry, Bill. We won't let you embarrass yourself." At that point I kind of breathed a sigh of relief. I knew they were great guys and that they would have my back.

About halfway home, I had a thought that made me break into a cold sweat: *If I'm on live TV and I say something stupid, how are these guys going to help me?* I figured I was going to be on my own, but I really

Jim Paschke was the perfect person to show me the ropes when I began my broadcasting career. *(Courtesy: Milwaukee Brewers)*

wasn't. Paschke helped me every step of the way. He was technically solid and still is as a broadcaster. I learned a lot from him. I'll never forget that he told me, "You don't want to be a player in the broadcast booth. You want to be a broadcaster that used to play in the big leagues."

That was a great lesson. There are things that you have to know, certain fundamentals in the broadcast booth, and one thing I learned over time was that you have to listen to your partner. That sounds really obvious. We're not two individual people working independently. We are a team. When I first started out, though, I was focusing so much on what I wanted to say that I sometimes stopped listening to what Jim was saying. I also had to learn my role. My job is not to dive into the media guide or the statistics sheet and talk about a guy being 5-for-7 with runners in scoring position on this trip. If the play-by-play guy brings that up, my job is to explain why a hitter is hot. Maybe he's doing a better job of staying back on the ball. He's not trying to pull the baseball in every at-bat. Maybe he's in a streak where he's not swinging at bad pitches. I learned that approach from Jim, but it took a while. There were times when he'd ask me a direct question, and I'd answer with something completely unrelated. I'm sure that I drove him nuts in the beginning. I would talk about random nonsense, and he would just look at me. As promised, he never embarrassed me on the air. He would, however, talk to me on the bus ride back to the hotel. At first I didn't understand. I thought he was supposed to do his thing and I was supposed to do my thing. It wasn't until the second half of my second year with Jim that I started to understand.

We started to get into a bit of a groove together, and I guess Jim reached a point where he had to make a decision whether he wanted to broadcast Bucks games or Brewers games. He elected to do basketball. Of all my partners, I think I learned the most from Jim. He's so solid in the fundamentals of television and baseball, and I owe my career to him. When I mention that to him, he says, "Don't pin that on me." He also has a good, dry sense of humor.

Jim was broadcasting when I was playing. He worked the Juan Nieves no-hitter that I caught in 1987 in Baltimore. He was working with Mike Hegan at the time and he got a lot of flack for not saying during the broadcast that Nieves was working on a no-hitter. Mike Hegan, another former Brewers player turned broadcaster, bought into the whole super-stition thing about no-hitters and Jim kind of went along.

That's always a tough call. When your pitcher has a no-hitter going deep into a game, a lot of fans want you to respect the tradition and avoid jinxing anything. In this age with Twitter and social media being so immediate, I think you need to bring it up. In fact if someone is flip-ping through the channels, they might not notice what's going on. You want to inform the audience.

Nowadays, most broadcasters will mention a no-hitter in prog-ress and take flack from fans if things fall apart. All you have to do is refer people to YouTube, where they can listen to legendary Dodgers broadcaster Vin Scully describe the final three outs of a Sandy Koufax no-hitter. If it's good enough for Vin Scully, it's good enough for the rest of us. Scully spent most of his career in California, the home state of my second partner, Matt Vasgersian, who would laugh at being mentioned in the same sentence—even tangentially—as the dapper Mr. Scully.

Matt Vasgersian

Matt joined the Brewers booth in 1997 and was with us for five years. We actually opened Miller Park together. The first year of the new ballpark was his last season. If you talk about a fundamental difference between broadcasters, going from Jim Paschke to Matt Vasgersian was like going from Nolan Ryan to Wilbur Wood. (Ryan was a hard-thrower, and Wood fluttered knuckleballs to the plate.)

Paschke was meat and potatoes guy, offering X's and O's and stuck to the game. We didn't get off on too many tangents or yuk it up too much. Vasgersian was the opposite. He was a Generation X guy and he loved funny stuff. He knew the game, too. He came up through the minor leagues and he knew what was going on. Both he and my current partner, Brian Anderson, worked in the Texas League. Vasgersian was with the Brewers' Double A affiliate in El Paso, Texas. Anderson was with the Dodgers' team in San Antonio. They became good friends and have plenty of funny stories about minor league road trips, equipment malfunctions, and the perils of being in the booth by yourself during long, boring games or rain delays.

Vasgersian was an innovator. He was a rebel in the broadcast booth. I always say that working with Matt was a roller coaster ride. You never know from one pitch to the next whether you were going to be talking about how to grip a slider or what happened on a classic episode of *The Flintstones*. He'd make references to The Great Gazoo and Bam-Bam and then he'd start talking about music that he liked. Matty has a deep love of music. I remember the Go-Go's were in Milwaukee one time, and we had them in the booth. All five of them were in there, and to this day, I don't know why. I think it's because the bass player, Jane Wiedlin, was born in Oconomowoc about 30 minutes west of the ballpark. So we had the Go-Go's in the booth, and Matt was excited about meeting Belinda Carlisle, the lead singer. The interview didn't go very well.

Another time, in Los Angeles, we had Jimmy Kimmel and Super Dave Osborne in the booth. Not only did we put them in headsets, but Vasgersian and I let Jimmy and Super Dave call the game. Chan Ho Park was pitching, and Kimmel was irreverent, as you can imagine, and he said something about people in Korea eating dogs. Needless to say, that didn't go over very well. We got our wrists slapped for that one.

Another time, Peter Frampton was in town, and Vasgersian had to have him on because he grew up listening to "Frampton Comes Alive," which was one of the biggest albums of Matt's childhood, even though Frampton had no connection to baseball. Matty wanted him and he came on the broadcast. Well, the Brewers were in the field at the time, and I think the team they were playing put up an eight-spot, and Frampton was on the air for about 25 minutes with Matty chatting him up about music and drummers and life on the road.

If you like Peter Frampton, that might have been your dream broadcast. A lot of people wondered if Matt was off his rocker. Of course, people wondered that more than once. There was a time in Miami back at Joe Robbie/Pro Player Stadium or whatever it was called at the time. Bobby Hughes, the Brewers' catcher who had gone to Matt's alma mater, USC, hit a high fly ball to left field, and it hit a clock at the top edge of the fence. It almost went out of the park. Vasgersian was doing the call, and his voice went up in anticipation of a home run, and without batting an eye, he said, "Bobby Hughes just got clock-blocked!" It was one of the funnier moments of my time with him.

When games would get boring, Matt had fun reacting to crowd

shots. One time, our director called up a shot of a family sitting wearing Nebraska Cornhuskers hats. They were like Cheeseheads—only with corn. Matty said, "Good to see the Corn-holers represented tonight." I nearly lost it. I have a million stories about my time with Matty—from on and off the air—and I'm not sure I can tell them all.

He may have been seen by some as a clown, but he loved the game and he was prepared. He obviously went on to bigger and better things, but he was—and still is—a cult hero in Milwaukee. He connected with a young generation of Brewers fans in a way that few announcers have done. By mixing in pop culture references, he made the broadcasts bearable no matter how things were going on the field. Bob Uecker, the legendary Hall of Fame radio broadcaster, is the same way. When the game is tight, he plays it straight. When the game gets out of hand, he has fun. By working with Matt, I realized that baseball is an escape. It's not life or death. After working with Jim Paschke in a no-nonsense way, it was good for me to be with Matt.

When we were in Seattle's Kingdome one time, Matty really needed tickets to the game—probably for somebody in Pearl Jam's road crew, but Dan Larrea, the Brewers' director of team travel, said he wasn't sure if he could get them. On the day we were leaving for Seattle, Matt and Dan crossed paths in the concourse, and Larrea said, "I think I can get your tickets in Seattle." Vasgersian responded, "That's okay. I went over your head and got them myself."

There are some people in baseball that you want to avoid making angry: the owner, the general manager, the umpire. And the traveling secretary is on the list along with the equipment manager. The traveling secretary is in charge of your meal money, your hotel room, and your luggage. He has a lot of power. Larrea didn't like what Matty said. I told Vasgersian he'd regret it. I told him to apologize, but he said, "It's no big deal."

A month later we got to Kansas City and we were staying at the Adam's Mark Hotel, a pretty dumpy place (by major league standards)

I stand next to Matt Vasgersian, who was a hoot to work with and very popular among viewers. *(Courtesy: Milwaukee Brewers)*

with the one redeeming quality of being located directly across the freeway from Royals Stadium. We checked into the hotel and went our separate ways, and the next afternoon on the bus to the ballpark, Vasgersian revealed that he was in a basement room with no windows next to a boiler room. He was sleeping on a lumpy murphy bed, and the boiler was making noise all night and he didn't get any sleep. Well, we found out weeks later that Larrea had set him up in that room and told the front desk not to allow him to move under any circumstances.

The next time we went to Kansas City, his room was right next to the bar, which was actually kind of a disco called Quincy's. They played loud music all night long. Vasgersian complained about how much he hated the hotel—and by extension every trip to Kansas City—and Larrea finally admitted, years later, that he had put him in crappy rooms as payback for going over his head in Seattle. Vasgersian was spitting mad when he found out. I think he still is. The rest of us laughed and high-fived Larrea for being devious enough to pull the prank and disciplined enough to keep it a secret.

From time to time, Vasgersian would go off to do a regional network game, and Len Kasper would come in and do games. I had been working with Len Kasper early on when he was with WTMJ and started doing the Sunday baseball show. Len had worked his way up through the ranks, starting at Milwaukee radio stations during his time at Marquette University. He would fill in for Vasgersian occasionally, and you could tell he had star potential. He went on to leave Milwaukee for the Florida Marlins job and then ended up in Chicago, where he'll be with the Cubs for years to come.

One particular time, for some reason, Matty left the Brewers before a series in Colorado, and there was no replacement. Jim Powell, who was working with Bob Uecker at the time, came over to the TV booth to help. Jim did the third, fourth, and seventh innings solo on the radio. When he was outside of those innings, he'd come over and do the TV. For some reason I ended up doing a lot of play by play and I had to do the third, fourth, and seventh innings. The game actually went into extra innings. It was the first time I'd ever worked alone in the booth. And if I remember correctly, the Brewers won the game.

I was a little nervous, but I think I did okay. Bob Uecker tells a story about the time early in his broadcasting career when his partners—Merle Harmon and Tom Collins—left him alone in the booth in the middle of an inning. "It was the only time I've ever been scared as a broadcaster," Uecker said. "Those guys walked out, and I thought they were kidding. I thought they were just playing a joke, and they'd be walking back in. I froze. After about a minute of dead air, which is a lifetime in baseball, I realized I had to start talking. I didn't know what to do. I talked about everything. I talked about paper on the floor of the booth. I talked about people in the stands. I got through it, though."

So did I.

Daron Sutton

After five years with the Brewers, Vasgersian moved on to San Diego. It was time for me to work with Partner No. 3. As usual the Brewers got a ton of inquiries from some very talented people. Daron Sutton emerged from the pack. Our director of broadcasting at the time was Tim Van Waggoner. When Sutton was auditioning, they decided to bring him in to the ballpark and have us do two or three innings of a mock broadcast to a tape of a game between the Brewers and the Chicago White Sox. We sat in the booth in the dead of winter with headsets on, doing a game from the monitors in the booth.

I could tell right away that it was going to be a good fit. Daron had a tie to Milwaukee because he'd spent time in the city when his father, Hall of Famer Don Sutton, pitched for the Brewers in the early 1980s. Daron had been doing radio with the Angels back in Southern California and worked on the pregame and postgame shows for the Atlanta Braves before that. He got the job and became my third partner in the booth. To this day I have never run into a guy with more energy and enthusiasm than Daron. He took every game to heart. He's one of those guys who sits in a chair, and his leg is thumping a mile a minute. He got to the ballpark early every day and stayed late. He always seemed like he had just chugged a gallon of the strongest coffee known to man.

He did every dinner. He did every season-ticket holder luncheon. He just couldn't get enough of connecting with fans. Actually, it was easy because Daron was a fan. When the team played badly, it was almost as though they were letting him down. Sometimes, he acted like they were doing it intentionally just to make him mad. I used to joke that Daron was getting paid by the word. My five years with him flew by because I didn't have to say a lot. I remember we would open the broadcast, and there were things that we were going to talk about. Usually, the play-by-play guy sets something up, and the analyst weighs in, and you go to break and get ready for the game. Daron would ask a question, then answer it. He'd ask another question, then answer that. He'd get to the third question, turn to me, and I'd have about 15 seconds to respond, and the opener was done.

Daron just loved the game so much. He wanted the team to succeed. If a pitcher like Ben Sheets was in the middle of a good game, our cameras would follow him off the field, and Daron would scream, "Let's get him some runs," as we went to commercial break. That wasn't an act. He really meant it. In all honesty, the Brewers weren't very good in the five years Daron and I worked together. The 2002 season, which was the worst in Brewers history, was probably my least enjoyable season in the big leagues. The team lost 106 games, and things weren't going well for the organization. That made it tough on Daron. It was tough on everybody.

Daron was emotional at times like that. His passion sometimes got the best of him, but his heart was always in the right place. He was as dedicated as could be, too. He'd get to the ballpark and talk to players—both Brewers and opponents. He developed great relationships with guys like Ken Griffey Jr. and others. He was a great "people person" and developed a rapport almost instantly. I liked watching him do that. I also learned from watching Daron that you can't take losses too seriously. You can't take it home with you. You just have to do the best job you can and realize that the outcome isn't in your control.

As much as I want the Brewers to win, I realize I don't have any control over it. When the team got to the playoffs in '08 and won the division in '11, it was a great relief. The pressure to get there was so strong.

I stand next to Daron Sutton, whose knowledge of the game was no surprise since his father was a great pitcher with the Brewers. *(Courtesy: Milwaukee Brewers)*

Although things haven't gone particularly well since 2011, it's easier to get through the bad times because of the successes in recent years.

Daron's exit from the club was a bit drawn out. There was a period when I thought he would return. He ended up moving to Arizona and working with the Diamondbacks, and the search was on for a new partner. I remember this was more of a tryout. We had a couple of guys in the finals and it was a two-day process. We did mock innings in a conference room.

Brian Anderson

Brian Anderson ultimately got that job. Brian and I are entering our 10th season together. That's longer than I've worked with any previous partner. He later reminded me that we had met before his audition.

Brian had worked with Matt Vasgersian in the Texas League. One thing about Vasgersian: he seemed to know more people than anybody possibly could know. He spent a lot of time in the minor leagues and he did a lot of things. It seemed like every city we visited, some minor league friend would get a credential and visit the booth for a bit and hang out with us for dinner in the press room. When we were in the Astrodome, it was Anderson who dropped by one time. I thought it was just another tag-along buddy who Vasgersian was dragging around. I thought he was being a bit of a big shot by getting these guys passes. Well, Brian reminds me that we ate dinner in the Astros press room and reminds me that I didn't give him the time of day. I just figured it was another of Matt's buddies. I might have been having a bad day. Maybe the fried chicken (a staple in the Houston press room) didn't agree with me. By the middle of the season and during a long road trip, you get tired of that stuff. Anyway, Brian says I "big-leagued" him, and I can't deny it.

But Brian has become a great, great, great friend. He's super talented obviously, which is evident to anybody who watches him do NCAA Tournament games or NFL games.

We hit it off very well right from the beginning. Brian is not a guy who tries to steal the spotlight. He allows me to do my thing and blends in. He's an awesome play-by-play man, because he's always very prepared. He has a good sense for the game of baseball because he played in college. His brother, Mike, was a big league pitcher and now works as a scout with the Texas Rangers. Like Brian, Mike is very highly thought of in the industry. One of claims to fame is that he pitched the game when Mark Whiten hit four home runs. I'm sure he'd appreciate me mentioning that, but he can always use a variation of the question I ask people: "When did you give up your home runs? I gave them up in the big leagues."

Brian has a vast background in broadcasting, and that is one of the things that makes him a special talent. He worked as a radio guy in the minor leagues for years, and those guys serve as their own producer/

engineer. On the TV side, he started out as a production guy. He pulled cables. He was a camera man. So he knows how cameramen think and try to weave the story of the game. He also knows how producers think and the ins and outs of a production truck. He was a sideline reporter for the San Antonio Spurs, so he knows what it's like to try and ask a coherent question when the crowd is roaring and you can barely hear yourself think.

Above all, Brian knows that in order to have a successful broadcast, everybody has to contribute. Brian does a great job of talking to everyone on the crew and making them feel important. There aren't many people who know what goes on in front of and behind the camera better than Brian does.

I talked to our director, Mark Vittorio, and producers, Brent Rieland and Brad Weimer, and they love the fact that Brian is very invested and involved in what content goes on the air. The people in our truck are fabulous, but they use Brian's knowledge and experience and they should. He's one of the best. The Brewers are very glad to have him, and he wants to be in Milwaukee. He makes no bones about that. We have a great rapport in the booth and off the field as well.

I've enjoyed working with all of my partners—and our crew people—and that's very important. Over the course of the season, you see your co-workers more than your family. In a way the crew is like a second family. People focus on the announcers, but there are a lot more people involved with putting on a broadcast than just the guys in the booth.

Director

Many of the players in the major leagues credit their parents with providing guidance, support, and inspiration on the path to the big leagues. Mark Vittorio is no different. Known as "Vito," Vittorio is director for Brewers broadcasts on Fox Sports Wisconsin. He credits his mother with pushing him toward the job. "I was a college student and I always loved television and I always loved sports," he said. "In the summer I was on academic probation and she said, 'Hey, what are we doing here? We're wasting time. You're wasting money. You're not motivated to be a good student.' I told her, 'I want to get into television, but everybody says it's the hardest field to get a job in.' She gave me great advice. She said, 'Who tells you that? The kids in the neighborhood? What do they know? Why don't you go to school for it and let them tell you that you can't find a job in the field? At least then you could say you tried.'"

With that, Vittorio transferred to a Columbia College, a Chicago school that specializes in radio/tv/film and set out to become a play-by-play guy. "I think everybody who starts out in the business wants to be on-camera," he said. "But as part of my curriculum, I had production classes and directing classes, and we were learning from people in the field. We were in Chicago. The people teaching were news directors at ABC. It was legit. As I started to get interested in every facet of television, I did a project and I directed it. I was at the school trying to check out some camera equipment for another project and I could hear the teacher talking to his class. It was the same teacher I had, but it was another class. He was pointing out certain things that he really liked that a student did. I could hear the music, and I knew it was my piece. It really got me thinking that I might be pretty good at it. That's when I shifted my focus on being a director. I was young. I was 22. That's kind of how I set out to do that."

The director sits in front of a monitor wall with upwards of 20 camera feeds staring at him. His job is to use those images to "paint a picture" of the game for people watching. "I won't say it's rocket science, but there is an art to it," Vittorio said. "I try to create a vision of what to put out there for the viewer and keep it in line with what the announcers are talking about."

Like the players on the field, TV directors in baseball are charged with making split-second decisions, and there isn't much room for error. Most baseball broadcasts rely on standard camera locations and designations.

- Camera 1 (low third base)—This camera on the third-base side shoots left-handed hitters and right-handed pitchers, so viewers can see players' faces. When a right-handed batter is at the plate, the operator at Camera 1 will focus on the runner closest to home plate and follow his journey. The low third-base camera also gets shots in both dugouts, both on-deck circles, and often follows players back to the third-base dugout.
- Camera 2 (high home)—This camera is located behind the plate. If you were shooting a game with one camera, this would be it. Camera 2 follows the ball more than anything else. It gets the appeal plays, check swings, and things like that. This camera also captures shots of runners, coaches, or the bullpen, but they're always focused on the pitch.
- Camera 3 (high first base)—This camera, sometimes located at "mid-first," often "shags" a close-up of players catching the ball. This is the camera that follows players after great plays or bad plays. They also get pick-off shots of runners on base.
- Camera 4 (center field)—This camera shoots from center field and shows every pitch, base hit up the middle, and stolen base attempts at second base. After a pitch this camera might zoom in on the batter (if he walks or strikes out) or the pitcher, who reacts to a result. This camera follows passed balls, wild pitches, and pop-ups behind the plate. On home runs this camera may follow the batter, the pitcher, or the spot where the ball landed in the stands.
- Camera 5 (low first base)—This camera is like a mirror image of Camera 1. It captures right-handed hitters and left-handed pitchers from the side. The operator also catches runners as they cross the plate.
- Camera 6 (high third base). This mirrors Camera 3 except it's on the opposite side.
- Camera 7 (tight center field) This operator shoots a tight head-

to-toe shot of the batter. If this is a "super slo-mo" camera, it can show the ball spinning out of the pitcher's hand or the ball impacting the bat.

- Camera 8 is the robotic camera often near the dugout, which is good for reaction shots in the dugout, the stands, and runners crossing the plate.
- Camera 9 (low home) is the low home plate camera at Miller Park.

"There is a formula to cutting the action," Vittorio said. "Every time the ball is pitched, that's Camera 4 in center field. Every time there is contact, that's Camera 2. Once the ball is in play, now you know it's still a little formulaic with showing the guy rounding third base. But then it starts to become an art. Are you using high home, so you can see the outfielder pick up the ball and throw it in? If you watch some games, you'll see a runner rounding third base, and they'll cut back, and the ball is already in the air. Sometimes, the fielder bobbles the ball. Now that gives a guy another base. You've got to be on top of that, and it's happening so fast.

"Let's say that there are men on first and second, one out. The batter steps up, and right before the pitch, I'll show the two runners from a high first-base position. That tells viewers there are two runners on. Here's the batter. I'll cut to the low first-base camera, and you'll see the batter take a warm-up swing. I'll cut to the pitcher. If it's a tense moment, we'll do a tight shot of him. As he's ready to pitch, I take Camera 4 in center field. If there is a ground ball up the middle, I'll stay with Camera 4 and let the ball come up the middle. Then, I'll take Camera 2 to get the runner rounding third. Then, I'll cut to Camera 5 to show the guy crossing home plate.

You've got to be careful, though, because these guys are awesome. "I got burned on a play in Atlanta because my camera guy was supposed to have more relativity, and the ball came in from right field. We had a man on first. There was a base hit to right, so I cut to Camera 2 (high home plate) for contact. Then, the high third position had a great look of the ball in the outfield and the guy running around second, coming in to third. So I took that camera and you could see the right fielder throw the ball in, and it was perfect. But our camera man wasn't shooting wide enough to know that he had to be the game camera now. And the Braves shortstop nonchalantly looked like he wasn't going to do anything, but he cut the ball off and threw behind the rookie runner and picked him off first base. I didn't cut to that, so I got burned. Those are the things you've got to be careful about. Over the course of a play, we might cut to five or six cameras in 10 seconds. I'll see a guy cross home plate. If the home team scores, I'll get a shot of the crowd. If the pitcher is backing up a base and walking back to the mound, I'll shoot him from the center-field camera to get his reaction. If a player made an error, I'll stay with him to get his reaction."

The director is in constant communication with photographers but also heads a crew that approaches 20 people involved with graphics, replay, and other things. "I talk way more than my announcers do during a game," Vittorio said. "You've got to know television and you've got to know the game. You have to understand the different nuances and the cadence of it."

On the front bench of the TV truck, you've got the producer, director, and technical director. Every camera, every tape machine, every source, and every graphic has a corresponding button. The technical director's role is to bring everything in and take it all out. There is the Fox Box, which shows the score and the count. There is Pitch Trax, there are two graphics channels and eight tape machines, and a myriad of effects that allow things to "dissolve" or fly from one element to another. The technical director listens to the director and hits the button.

At the crack of the bat, the director can say "Camera 2," and the technical director will push the button that makes Camera 2 go live (with a red light glowing). The director will give cues to "Take Camera 5" followed by

"Ready Camera 3" and "Take Camera 3." He'll also say, "Ready to replay to X, fly to X," and the technical director makes his vision happen."

On the back bench of the truck, the graphics coordinator, graphics operator, and Fox Box operator sit. In the tape room, you have four tape operators and one or two engineers. Everybody has a job to do and everybody can make a broadcast better. When you pull into the South Dock at Miller Park, you'll see the home TV truck next to the visiting TV truck. When a series begins with a night game, the truck will pull in at about 11:00 AM for the park and power part of the day. The engineer will show up, plug the truck in, and get the Internet working. At 12:30 PM there is a crew call. The camera guys show up, open the side bins, and start pulling out the cameras.

Everybody sets their equipment up. The producer has a hard drive with all the video elements and highlights that will be used to tell the story for that game. The director will call in to Fox and make sure the phone lines are working. There are six lines that come in and out of the truck, connecting it to master control and other entities. At 3:00 PM all the cameras are checked, along with the headsets. After that the crew goes to lunch and maybe has a pre-production meeting. If there are "billboards"—the ads used in the opening of broadcasts and coming back from break—those can be voiced and recorded. Everything comes through the truck, which is the hub of activity.

Producer

Brent Rieland, who is the producer for Brewers games on Fox Sports Wisconsin, works with the director to manage the crew and present the action. In some ways the producer is like the coach, and the director is like the quarterback. The producer can call a play, but the quarterback can change it at the line of scrimmage. "The producer has a vision of the show, and the director executes it," Rieland said. "The producer has a list of things that have to happen—promo announcement, sponsors, and elements that have to get on the air. There might be 20 things that need to get in, and you don't want to jam them in where they don't belong," Rieland said. "Essentially, the producer helps the director between pitches. The producer can help with the replay sequences. The producer talks to the announcers and the sideline reporter. The producer says, 'We're going to come back from commercial with a highlight package of Ryan Braun' and then we're going to go to the pitch.'"

The producer comes up with the scenic shots that open the broadcast—video of the stadium, the cityscape, fans coming through the gates or shots of key players warming up.

When the game starts, the producer keeps the show flowing. If Ryan Braun has three hits in his first three at-bats and is on deck, the producer tells tape operators to have replays of the three hits ready. When Braun comes to the plate, those replays will roll to set the stage for the fourth at-bat.

The sideline reporter, Sophia Minnaert and Telly Hughes, listen to the broadcast from the photo well near the dugout. If Brian Anderson and I talk about a player, Sophia can tell the producer something she heard before the game and he will bring her into the show—usually as a batter is walking to the plate.

The advent of replay reviews in Major League Baseball has impacted life in the TV truck.

"We feel a responsibility and a sense of urgency to get a definitive look at a play, especially if your manager is trying to reverse something," Vittorio said. "Let's say that Jean Segura makes a diving play deep in the hole and barely gets the runner. We're not showing the dive. That's an afterthought. We want to know if the runner is safe or out."

In addition to following the flow of a particular game, the producer has to think about where each game fits into the bigger picture of the season. If a team is suffering from an epidemic of injuries, the producer will create a montage of players being hurt and replacements warming up. "We have a conference call at 10 every morning to discuss story lines," Rieland said. "If Ryan Braun has four homers in his last five games, that's a story. If Jonathan Lucroy pulled a hamstring running to first the previous night, we have to be ready to talk about it and maybe have video of the play and of his backup during warm-ups."

Producers usually start their career as a production assistant (PA). "A PA is usually working for the producer, doing a lot more video editing," he said. "It's more lower-level work and following the producer's orders. You're basically told what to do, and it's hands-on work."

From there, Rieland worked his way up to postgame show producer and into producing games. "The most difficult part of the job is balancing things out," he said. "The producer and director are in charge of tape, audio, graphics…It's hard to balance everything and not focus on one end and lose track of the other end."

When people visit a TV truck for the first time, they're usually blown away by what goes on in a cramped space. "It changes the way they watch games at home," Vittorio said. "The teamwork and communication and the replays. Once they see what goes into it, they'll never watch games the same way again."

Calling Pitches

One of the most common questions I get from fans who watch Brewers broadcasts is, "How do you know right away what pitch just fooled that hitter or got pounded off the wall?"

Part of how I know is that I've been doing it for so long. I was a catcher from the age of seven years old and I've been watching pitchers and catchers all my life. It's not rocket science, but there is some thought that goes into it.

It begins with pregame preparation. I use a program on the computer where I can punch in a pitcher's name, and it will give a little bit of a biography. Part of that summary is the pitches that he throws. That's a good starting point, but the information there is sometimes outdated and in rare cases flat-out wrong. If I'm doing a spring training game, and a kid comes up from Double A and I have no information on his repertoire, I'll use that profile to give me a quick background. It might say that he has a good fastball, rushing it up there in the mid-90 mph range, a slider, and a developing change-up.

When the season starts, I don't do a lot of that. I know the Brewers pitchers from watching them throw every night. It's different with the opponents. If a guy throws a slider, a split-finger fastball, and a change-up, you don't want to misidentify the pitches. You don't want to say, "He's got a good splitter" and then find out he doesn't throw one. A lot of times, I'll go down and talk to Darnell Coles, the hitting coach, to get a sense of what the pitcher that day is throwing. If it's Clayton Kershaw throwing for the Los Angeles Dodgers, I know he's got a big curveball and will throw a lot of cut fastballs. If it's Jonathan Niese from the New York Mets, I have a sense of what he does, but I'll ask the hitting coach what he likes to do in certain situations. I'll ask: "Does he attack inside early in the count? During the second time through the order, does he try to work away? With men on base, does he soften up and go with sliders and change-ups?"

We have computer programs that show that 72 percent of a guy's first-pitch fastballs are strikes. When he gets ahead, 72 percent of his sliders are out of the strike zone. You can get a sense for how a guy throws without seeing him pitch. When the game starts, I will watch the monitor to identify pitches. Brian Anderson is done with the monitor when the pitcher starts his windup because Brian has to call the action. I'll stay with the monitor and see the pitch and where it ends up in relation to where the catcher set the target.

If the hitter makes contact, I'll look at the Fox Box for the speed of the pitch. If it says 83 mph, I'll know it was a change-up. Generally speaking, pitches that are 90 mph or faster are fastballs, and pitches that are in the low 80-mph range are curveballs or change-ups. Sometimes, you can tell by the way the hitter reacts. If he's way out in front and yanks it foul, it was probably an off-speed pitch. If he swings late and barely makes contact, it was probably a fastball.

You can also make an educated guess about a pitch by the count. A lot of pitchers, particularly relievers, will throw mostly first-pitch fast-balls. If a pitcher is behind 2–0, he'll often throw a fastball to try to "get back" in the count. A 1–2 pitch is a good spot to bury a breaking ball and try to get the hitter to chase.

Once I see contact, I'm watching to see if the pitch was up or down and in or away. Then my eyes will move to the field to see what I want to talk about as the play develops. If someone hangs a curveball, and it's a simple base hit, that's what I'll talk about. If he hangs a curveball and Carlos Gomez makes a great sliding catch and throws a guy out on the bases, that's what I'll talk about.

Sometimes, you'll see a number of replays. I might talk about the pitch, the selection, location, or execution. I might talk about the ball going into the outfield. I might talk about where Scooter Gennett is posi-tioned at the bag, how he catches the ball, and how he applies the tag. Does he reach for the runner? Does he drop his glove right by the bag? Those are things I'll discuss. On a swing and a miss, if I make a big deal about the pitch and it was a great location, the guys in the truck know I'm interested in that, and they are going to call up a replay. We'll see Jonathan Lucroy set up on the outside corner. We'll see the target. We'll see the pitcher put the ball right on the money. And we go from there.

The last thing I'm going to do is say the same thing Brian Anderson just said. If Brian says, "Ground ball to third. Herrera up with it, over to first, two outs." I have to point out that Joe Blow just rolled over on a slider and made it an easy out. I'll talk about waiting back on the breaking ball. I'm not big on numbers. Anderson might say that Ryan Braun is 7-for-9 against Niese with three home runs. My job is to say why Braun hits lefties well. Niese doesn't have a lot of velocity. At Miller Park, well-hit balls often leave the park.

ACKNOWLEDGMENTS

Bill Schroeder

My life in baseball—as a player and broadcaster—wouldn't have been possible without the support and sacrifice of my parents, Pete and Carol, and family, Kate, Lindsey, Billy, and Mallory. I love you all.

I'd also like to thank the Milwaukee Brewers organization, which has been like a second family to me since the day I was drafted in 1979. I owe a debt to all of the managers, coaches, teammates, trainers, clubhouse attendants, front-office employees, and stadium workers who have treated me so well over the years. The ones who have provided me with so many memories.

Thanks to the Selig family—Bud, Wendy Selig-Prieb, and Laurel Prieb—for being great to me over the years and giving me a chance to stay connected to the organization after my playing days. And thanks to current owners Mark and Debbie Attanasio, along with Rick Schlesinger, Tyler Barnes, Aleta Mercer, Tim Van Wagoner, and others for their generous and unwavering support. I can't imagine doing this for any other team.

Thanks to all the broadcast partners I've shared the booth with over the years—Jim Paschke, Matt Vasgersian, Daron Sutton, Brian Anderson, Len Kasper, Craig Coshun, and Matt Lepay—for their patience and friendship. Thanks to our directors, producers, and crew members who have tried to make me look and sound good over the years, especially our excellent team at Fox Sports Wisconsin.

Thanks to Bob Uecker for his advice and support through the years. And to the people behind the scenes, who helped so much with this book—Tony Migliaccio, Dan Larrea, Joe Crawford, Dan Wright, Jason Shawger, and others.

Finally, I'd like to thank the Brewers fans, who have put up with 21 years of my nonsense in the booth. I'll even thank the ones who booed me as a player because without that passion the job wouldn't be as fun.

Drew Olson

When I started covering the Brewers beat for the *Milwaukee Journal* in the strike-scarred winter of 1994, one of the first stories I wrote was about Bill Schroeder becoming the team's new TV analyst.

Two decades later, here we are…

Thanks to Rock for devoting so much time and energy to this project and making my job easy. Thanks for all the people who contributed their time and stories—some of which we saved for the next book.

I'd also like to thank my parents, Roger and Dorie, for making me focus on my English homework rather than misguided dreams of playing sports for a living; my sisters, Amy and Annie; and, my wife, Barb, and daughter, Aubrey, for keeping dinner warm while I worked on this project and a zillion others. Thanks to our dogs, Magic and Burton, for acting happy to see me when I did get home.

I'd also like to thank all the managers, players, coaches, scouts, broadcasters, technicians, stadium workers, and, especially my fellow baseball writers, for making every day at the ballpark seem more like vacation than work. I'd like to offer a special thanks to Tom Haudricourt for years of friendship, advice, and laughter. He had a front-row seat for many of these stories, and his knowledge of the Brewers is unparalleled.

SOURCES

Newspapers

Milwaukee Journal

Milwaukee Sentinel

Milwaukee Journal-Sentinel

Arizona Republic

Chicago Tribune

Chicago Sun-Times

Los Angeles Times

Racine Journal-Times

St. Louis Post-Dispatch

The Baltimore Sun

The New York Times

The Seattle Times

The Washington Post

Magazines

Brewers Yearbook

Brewers GameDay

Sports Illustrated

Sport Magazine

Baseball Digest

Websites

Brewers.com

Baseball-almanac.com

Baseball-reference.com

Blearcherreport.com

CBSsports.com

ESPN.com

MLB.com

SABR.org (Society of American Baseball Research)

Sbnation.com

Wikipedia.com

Books

Where Have You Gone, '82 Brewers, Tom Haudricourt

Brewers Essential: Everything You Need to Know to Be a Real Fan, Tom Haudricourt

100 Things Brewers Fans Should Know & Do Before They Die, Tom Haudricourt

Throwback: A Big-League Catcher Tells How the Game Is Really Played, Jason Kendall and Lee Judge

The Game Behind the Game: Negotiating in the Big Leagues, Ron Simon

Video

Midwest Sports Channel

Fox Sports Wisconsin

Harvey's Wallbangers: The 1982 Milwaukee Brewers (DVD)

Magic, Miracles, and True Believers (VHS)